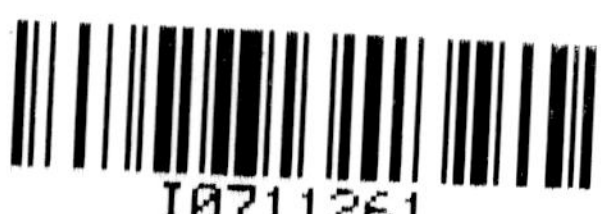

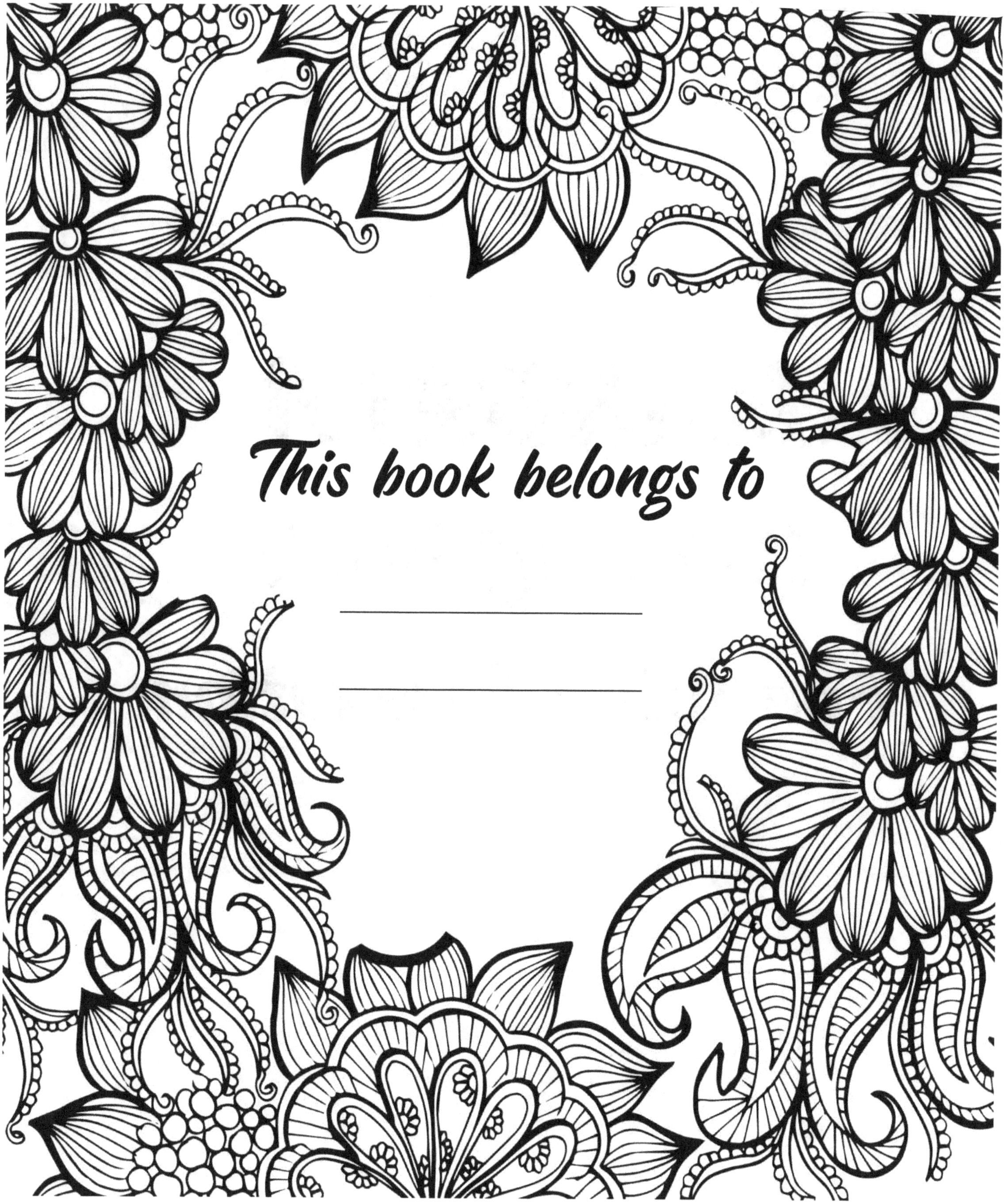

This book belongs to

____

____

MANDALA
Coloring Book
For Adult Relaxation

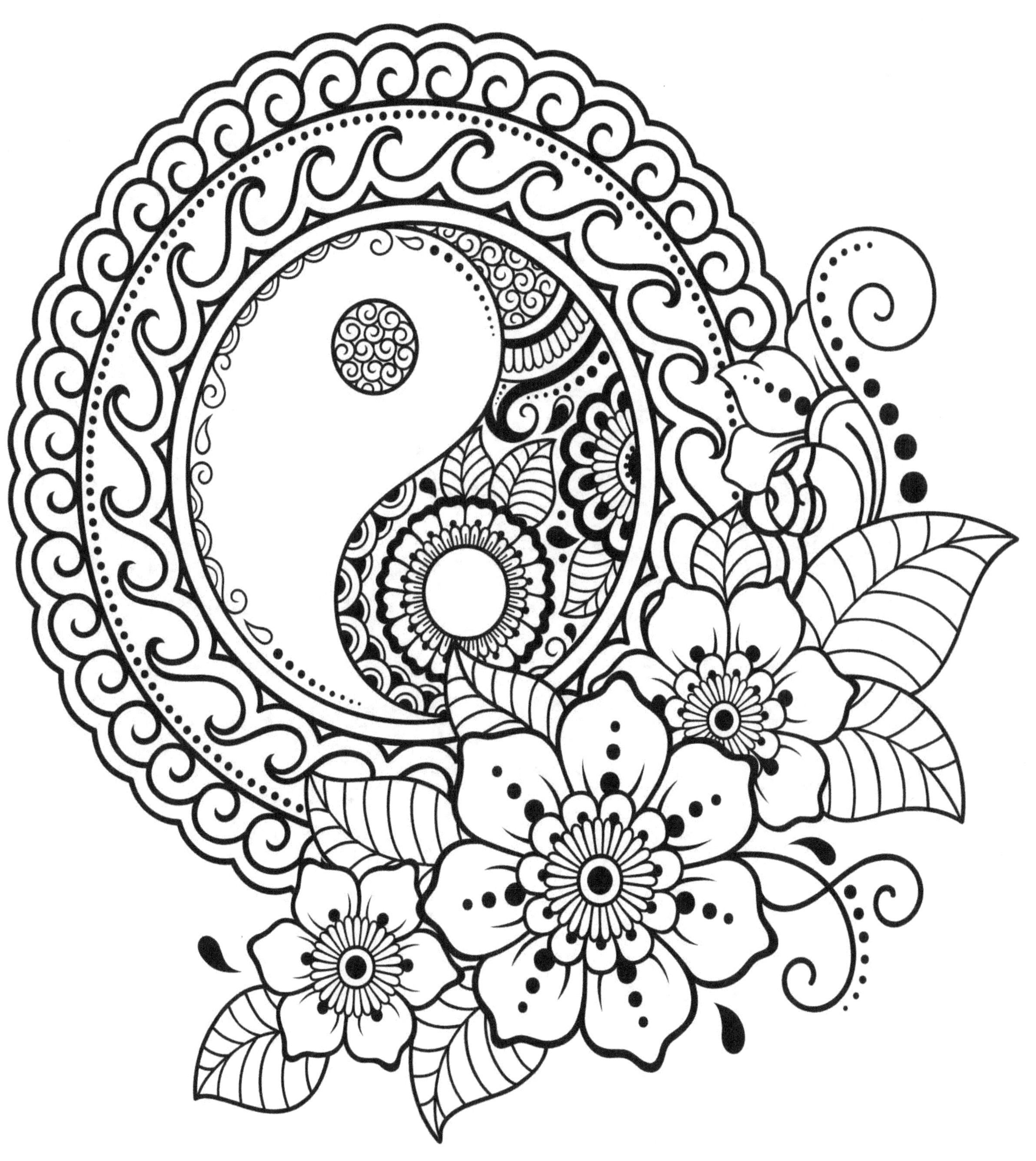

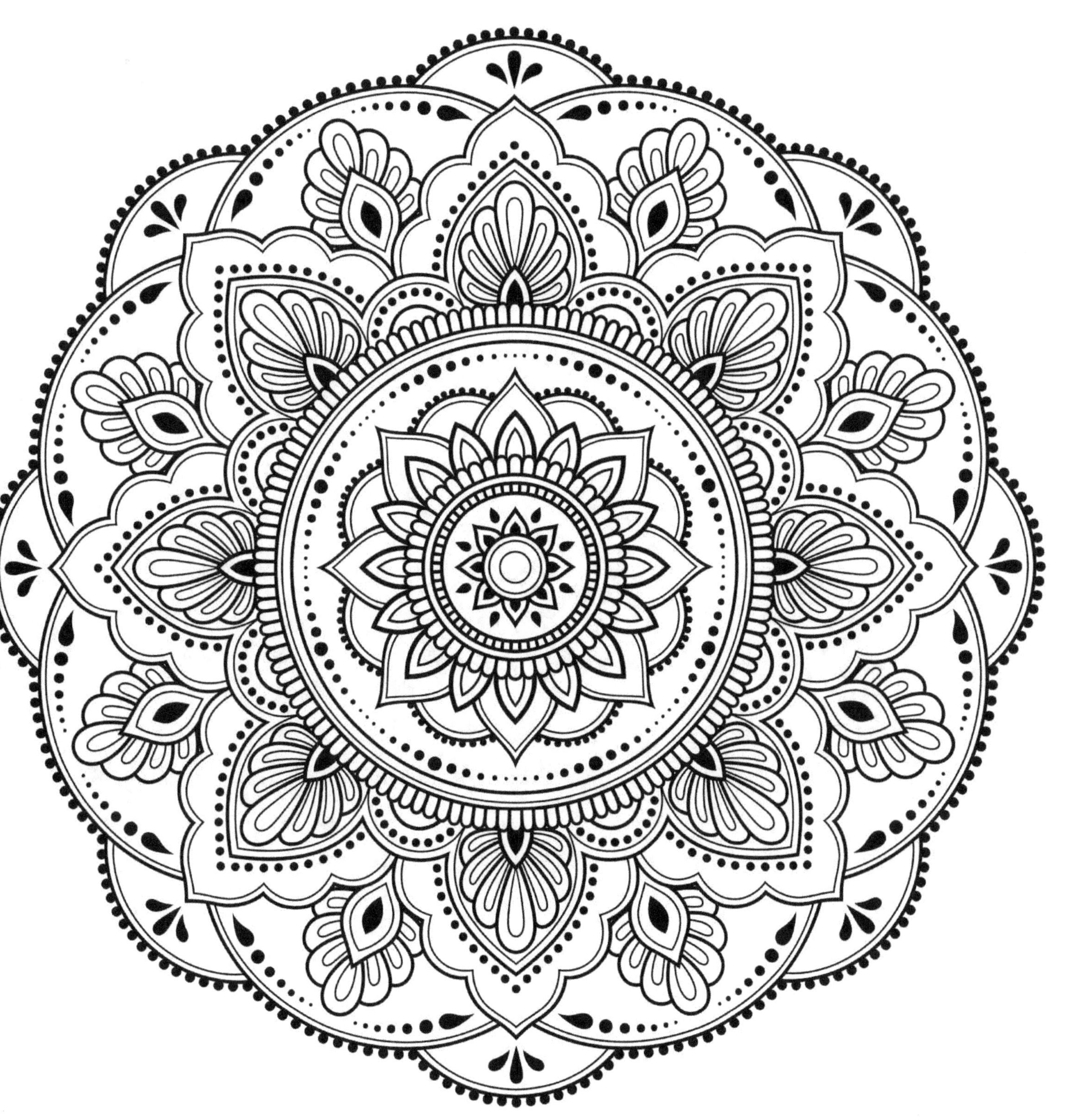

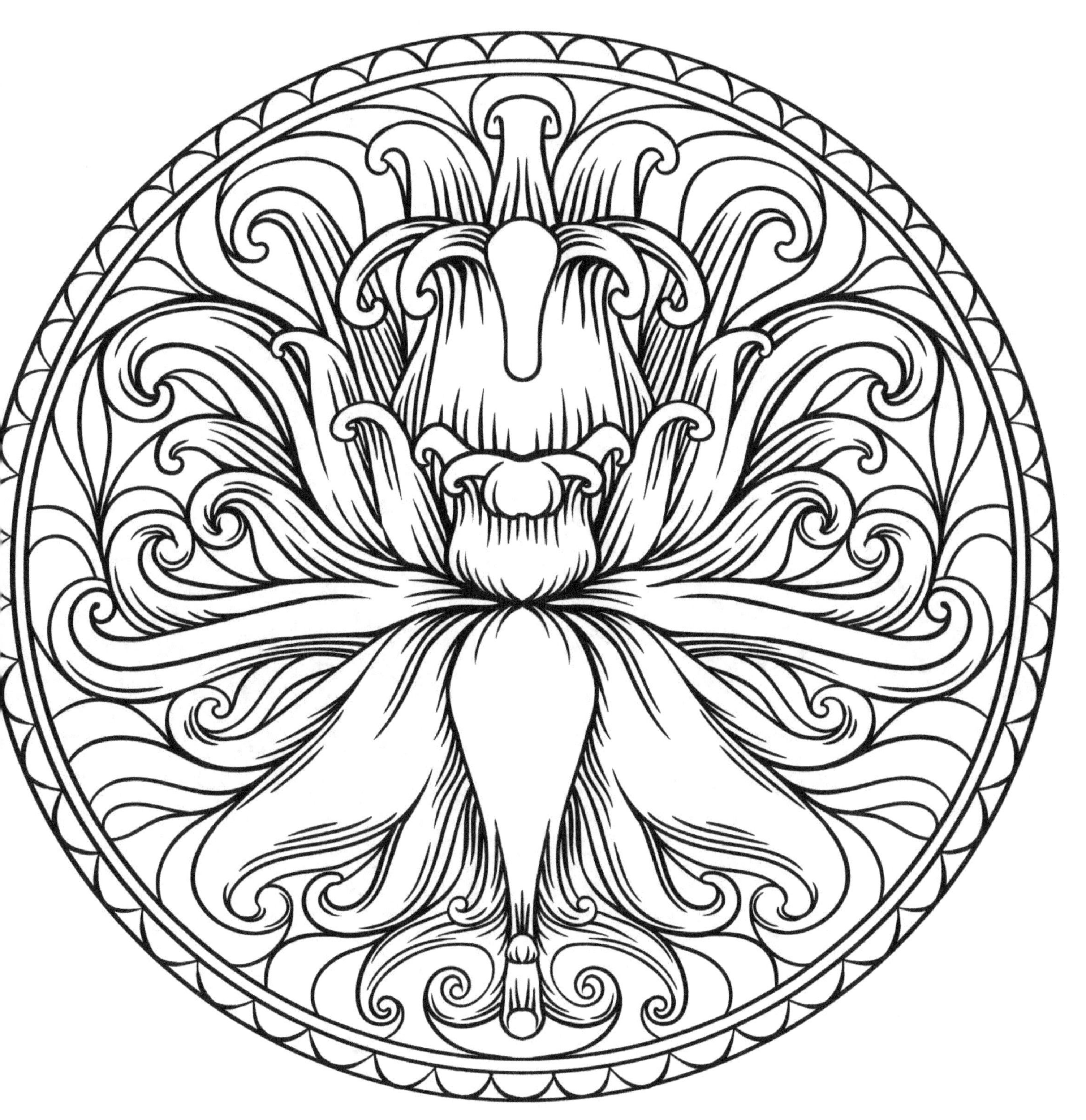

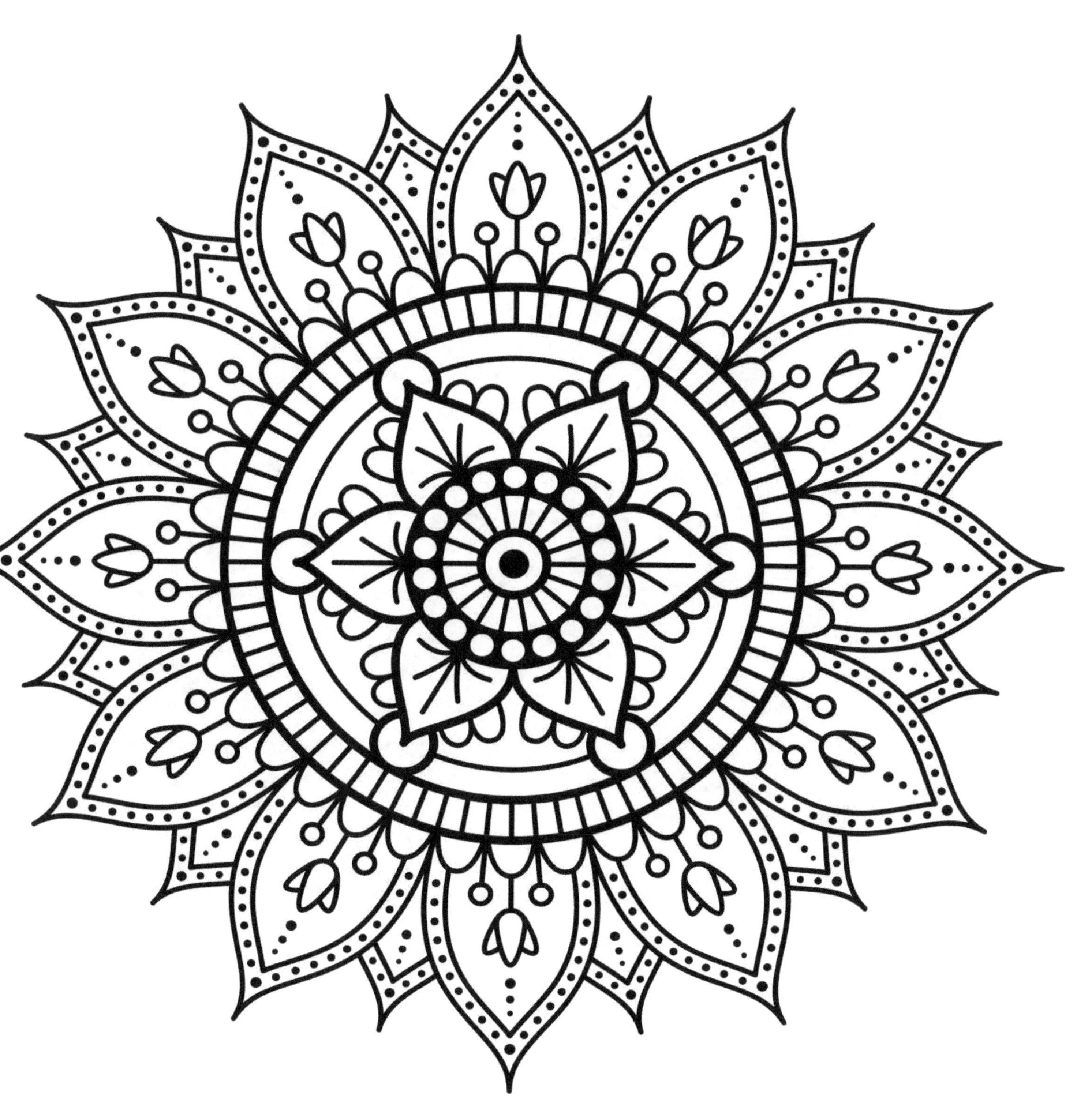

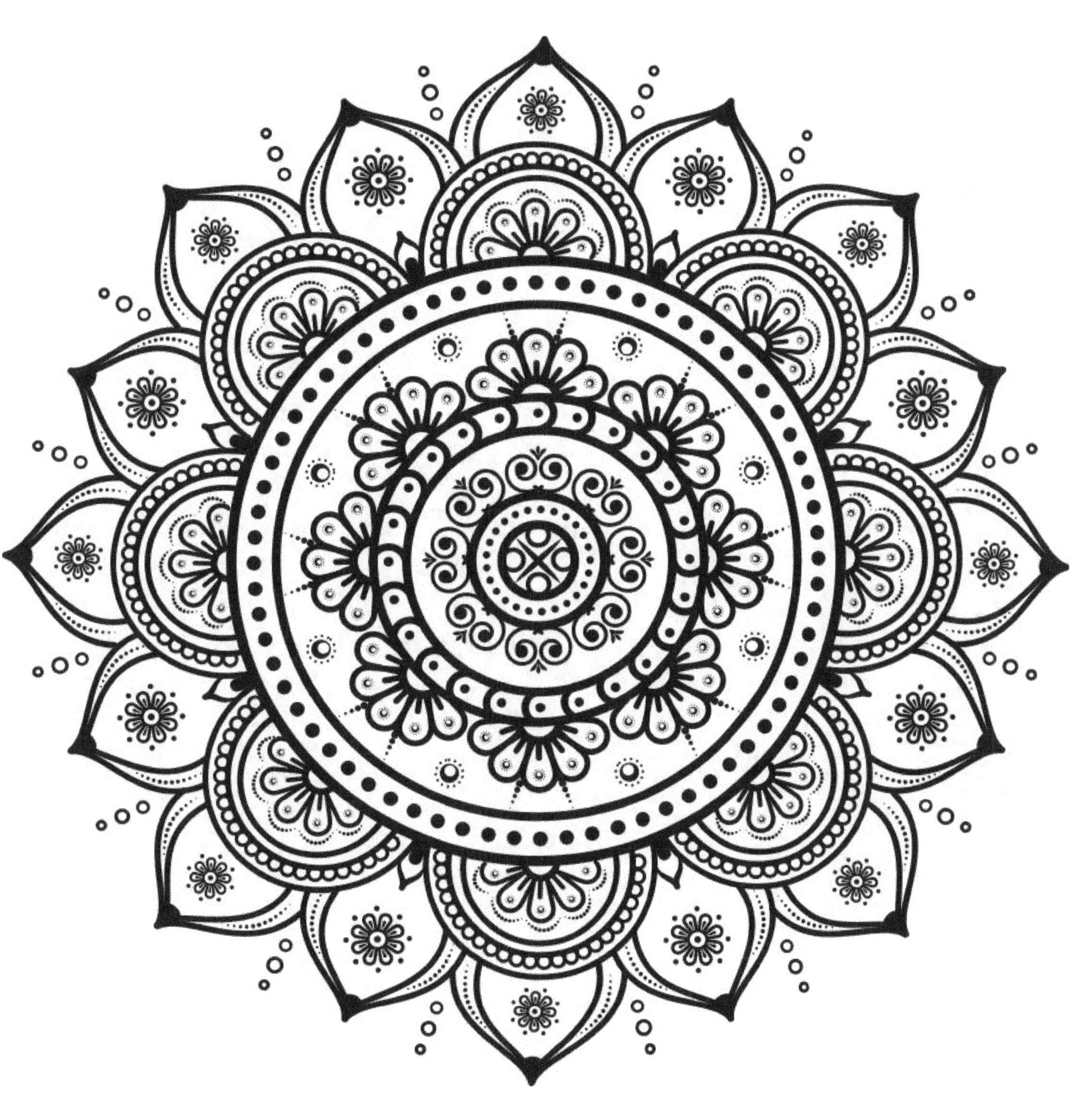

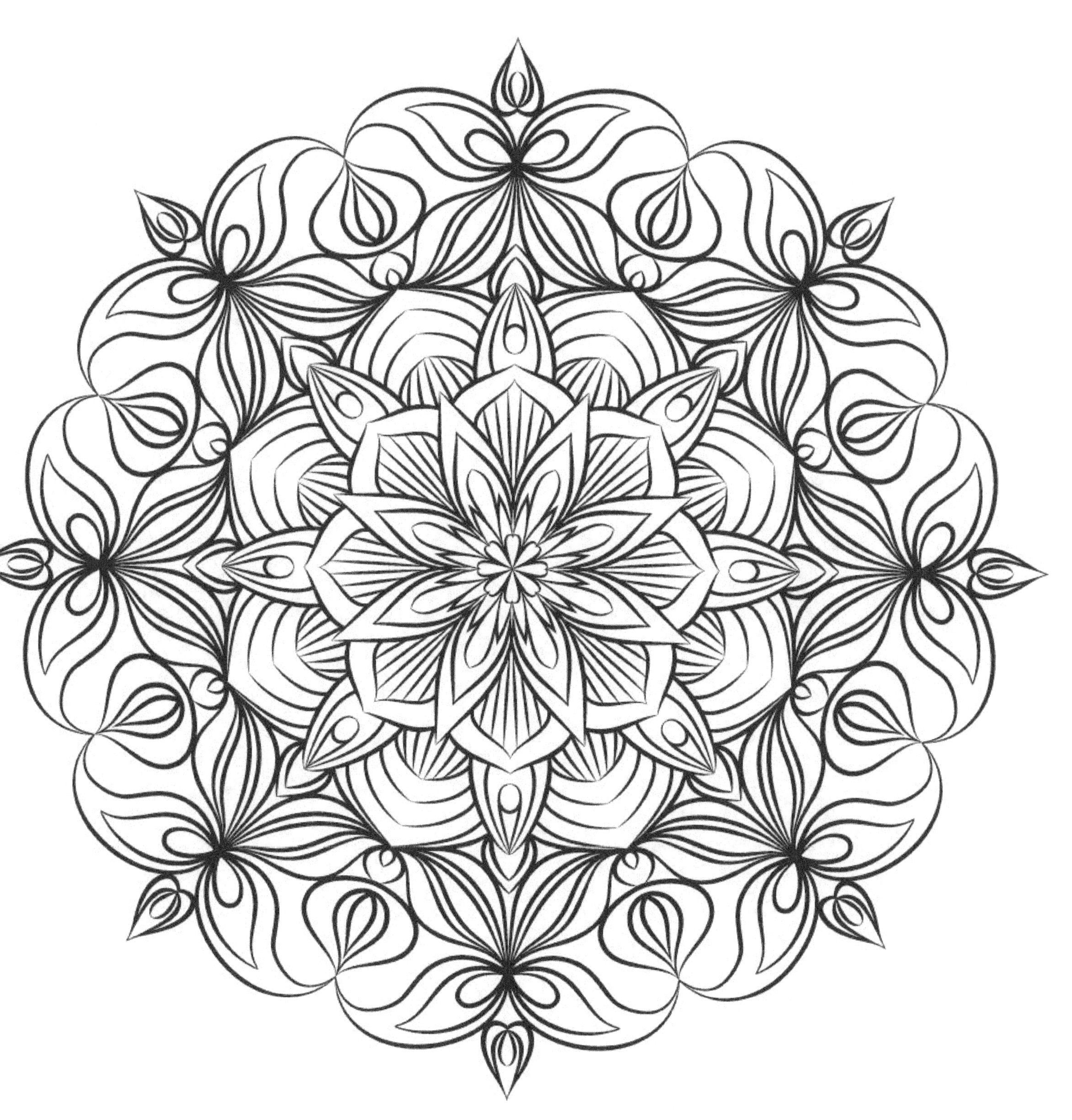

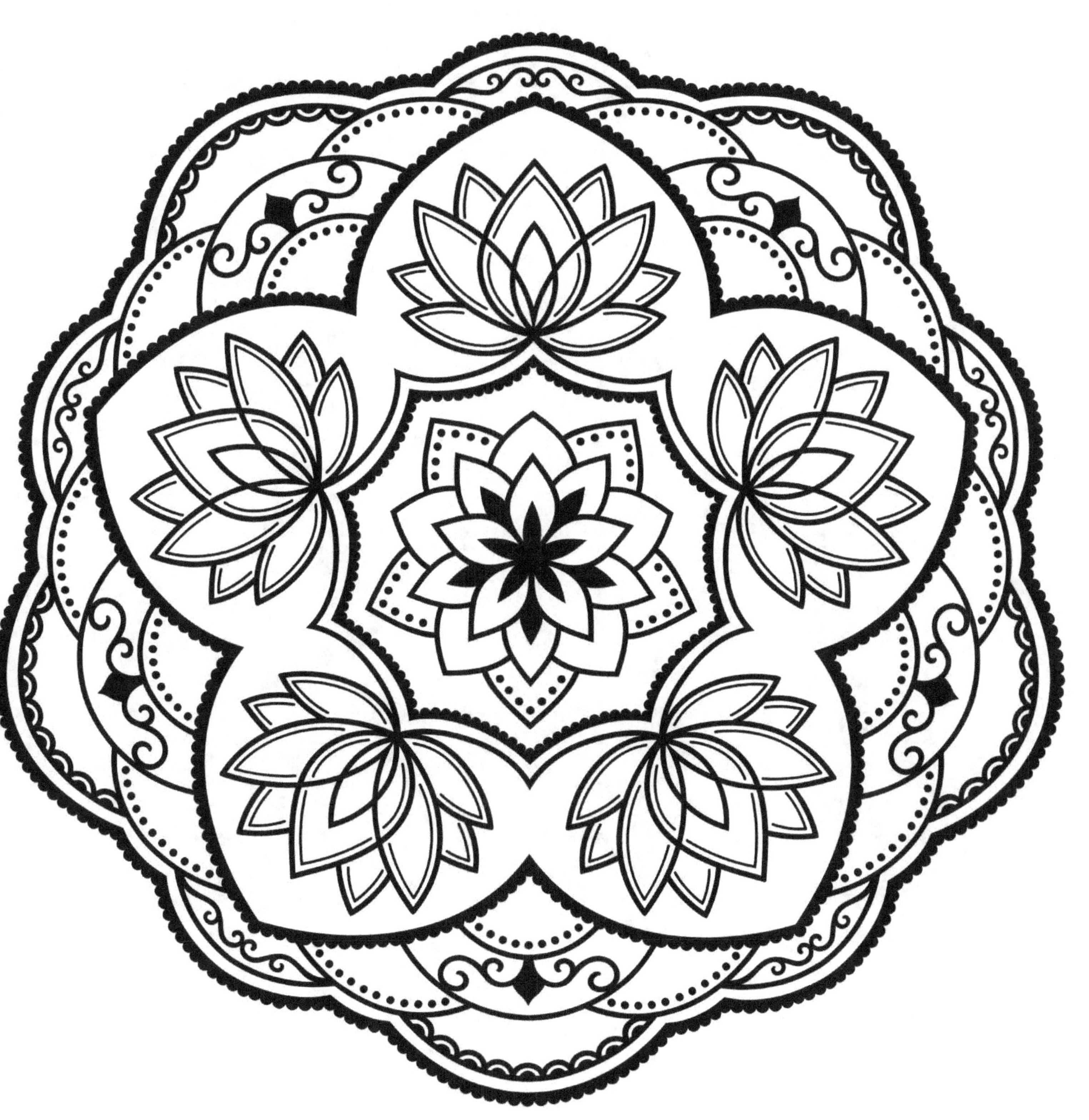

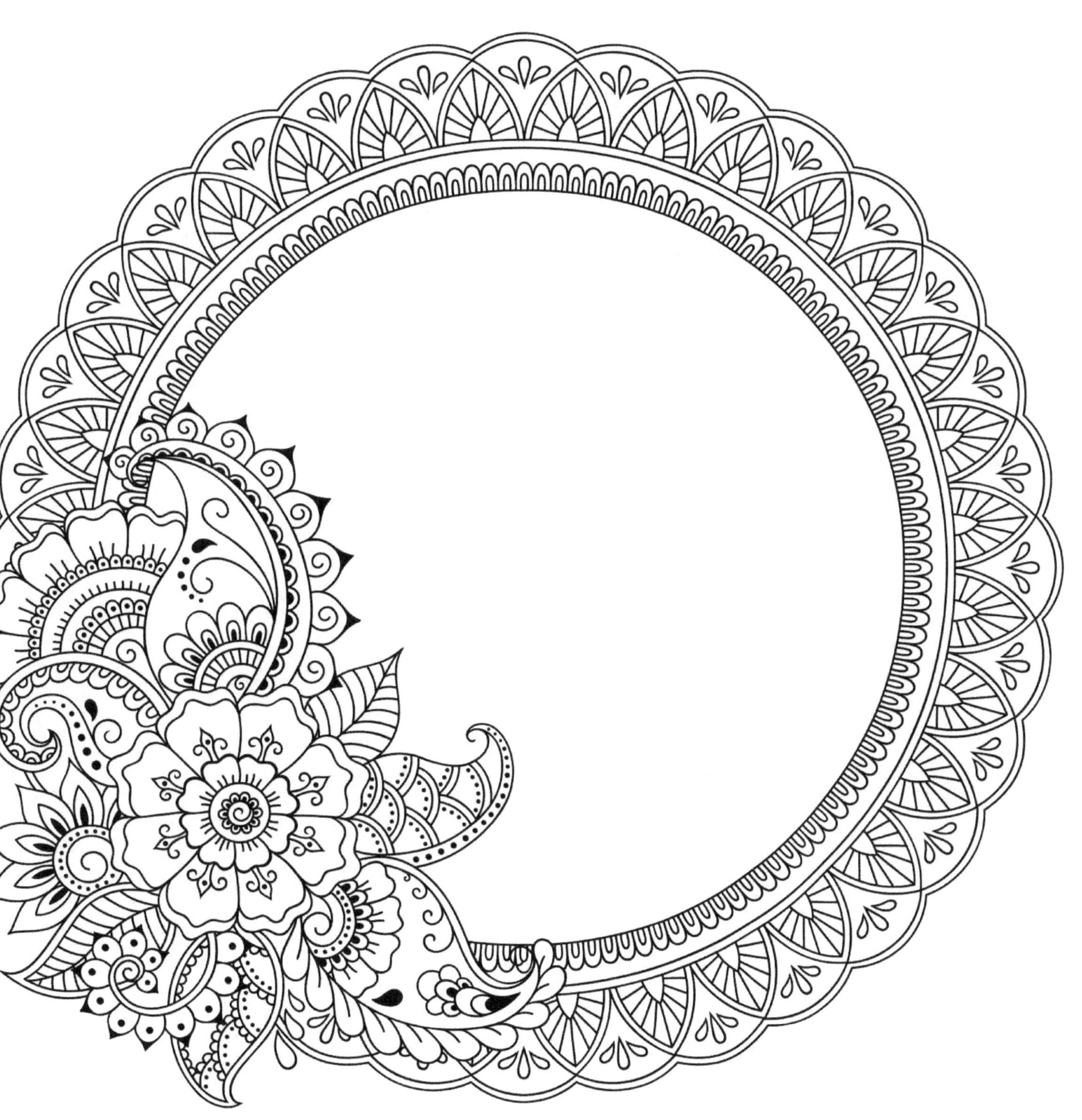

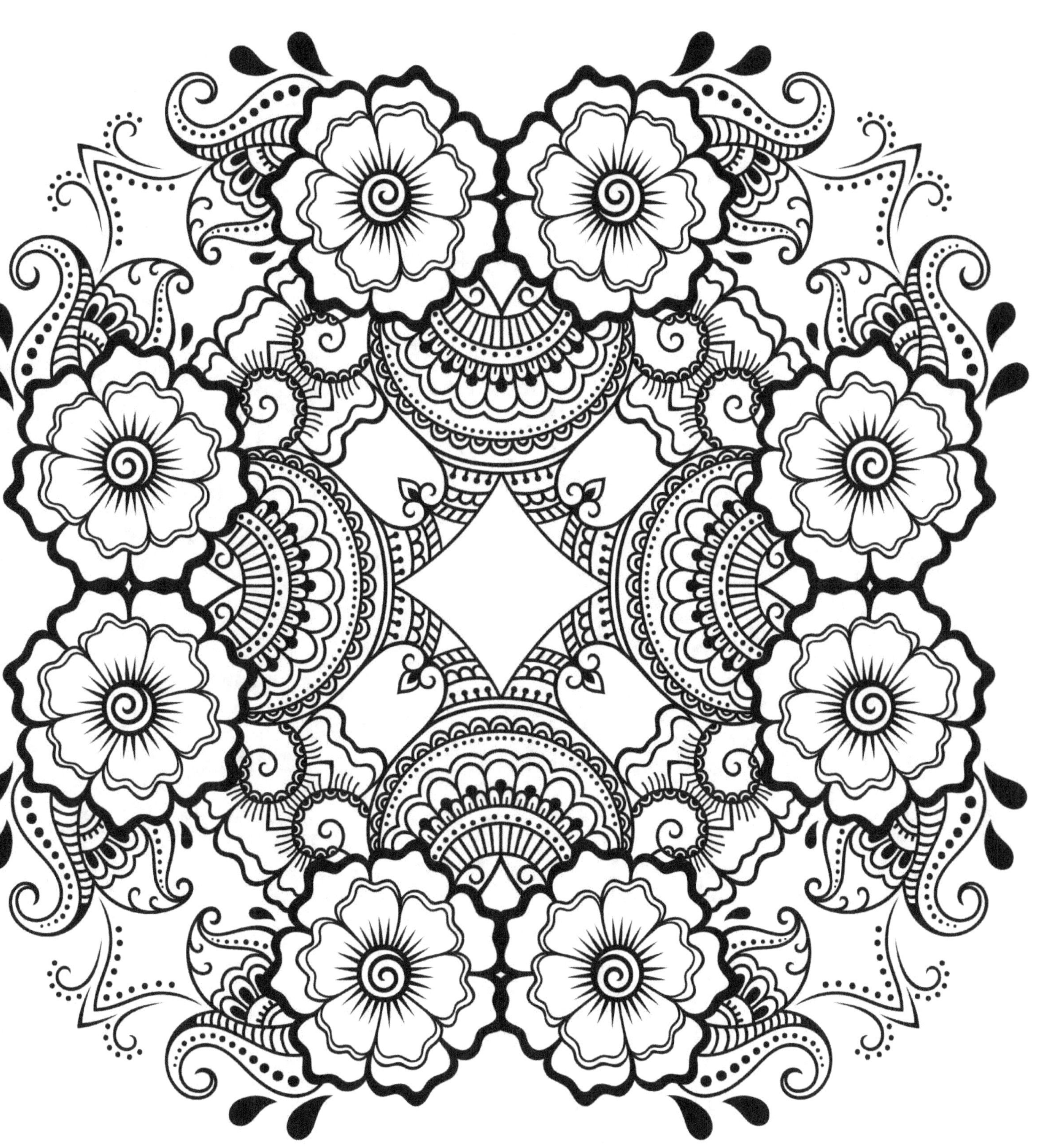

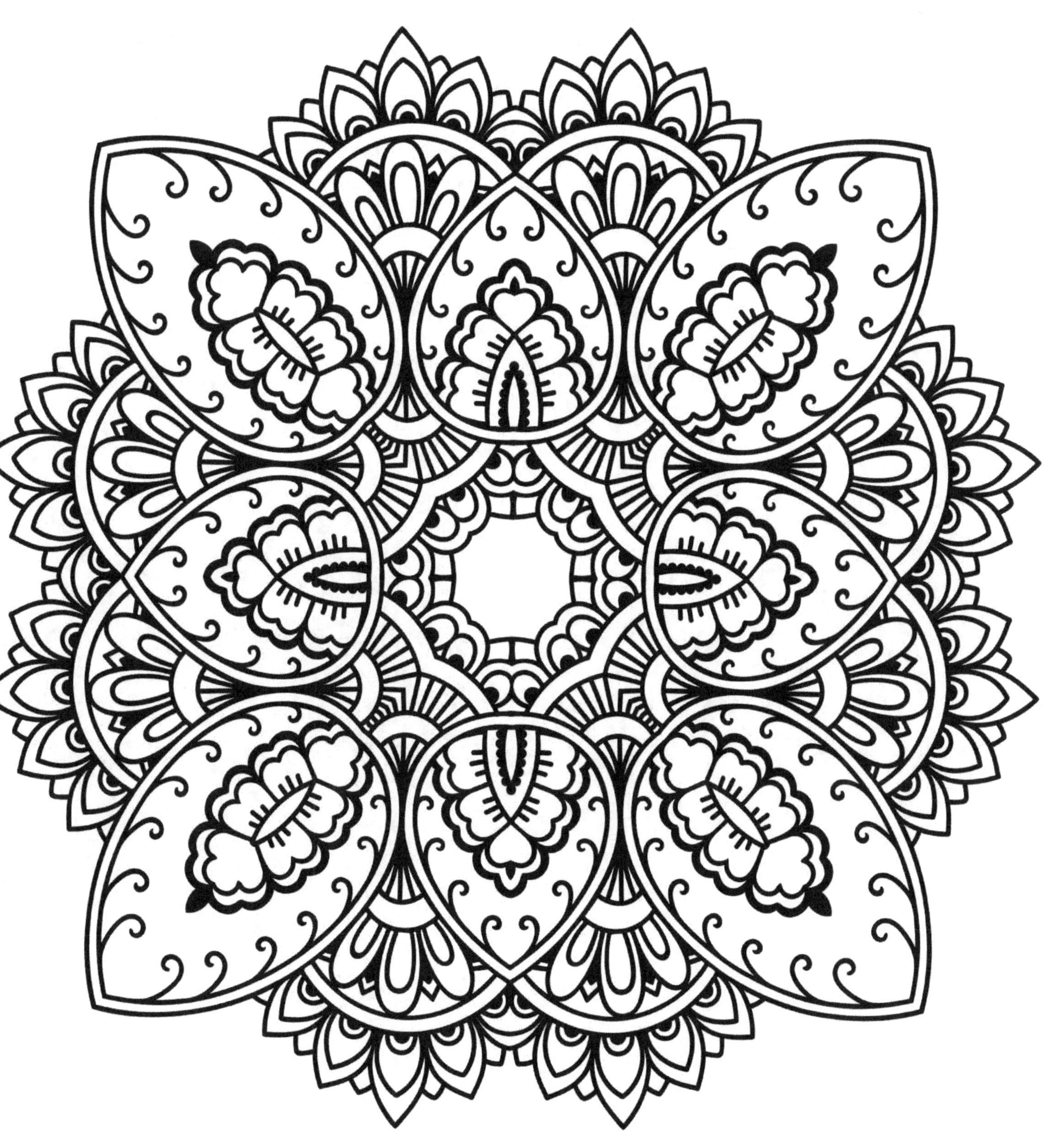

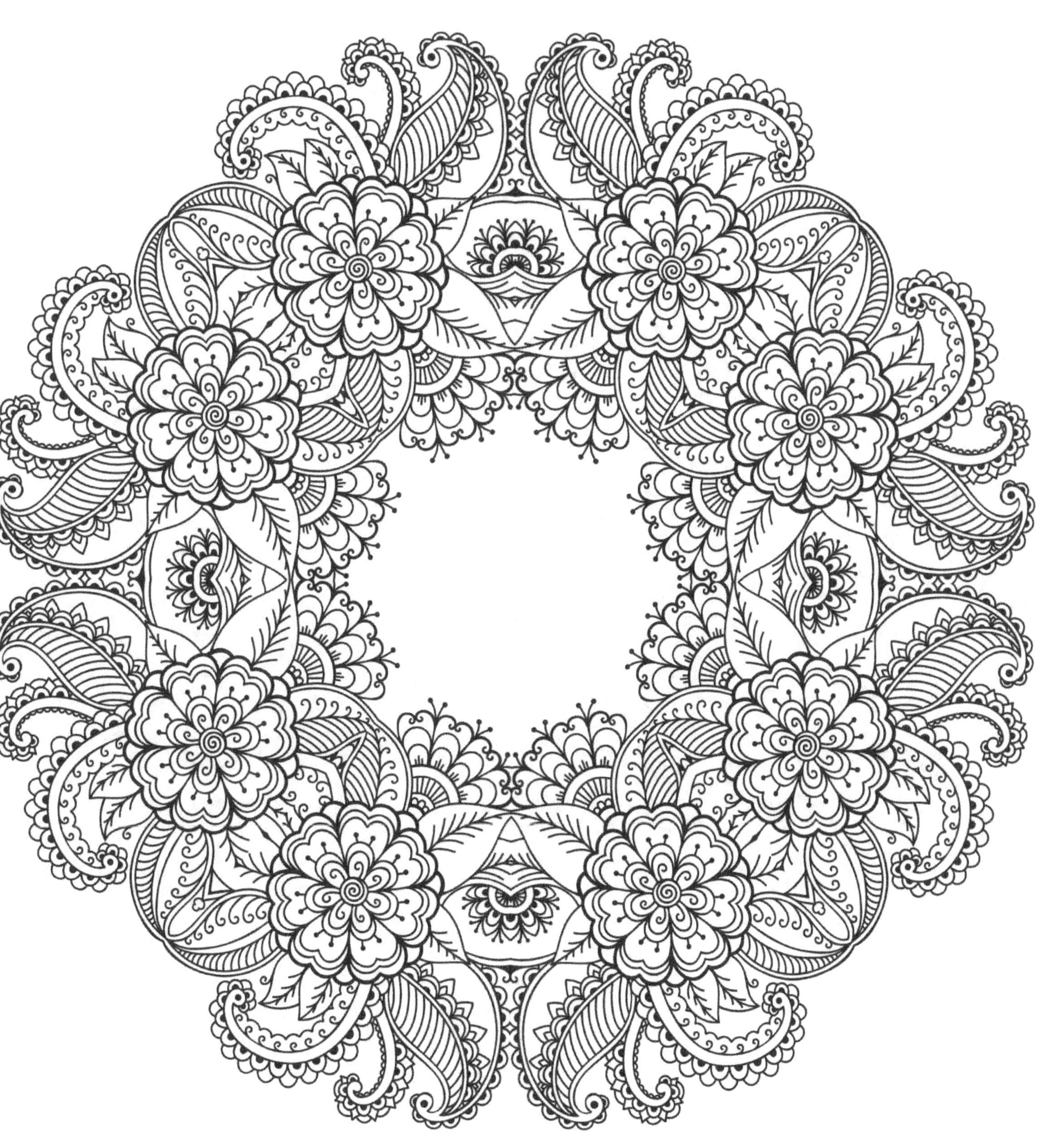

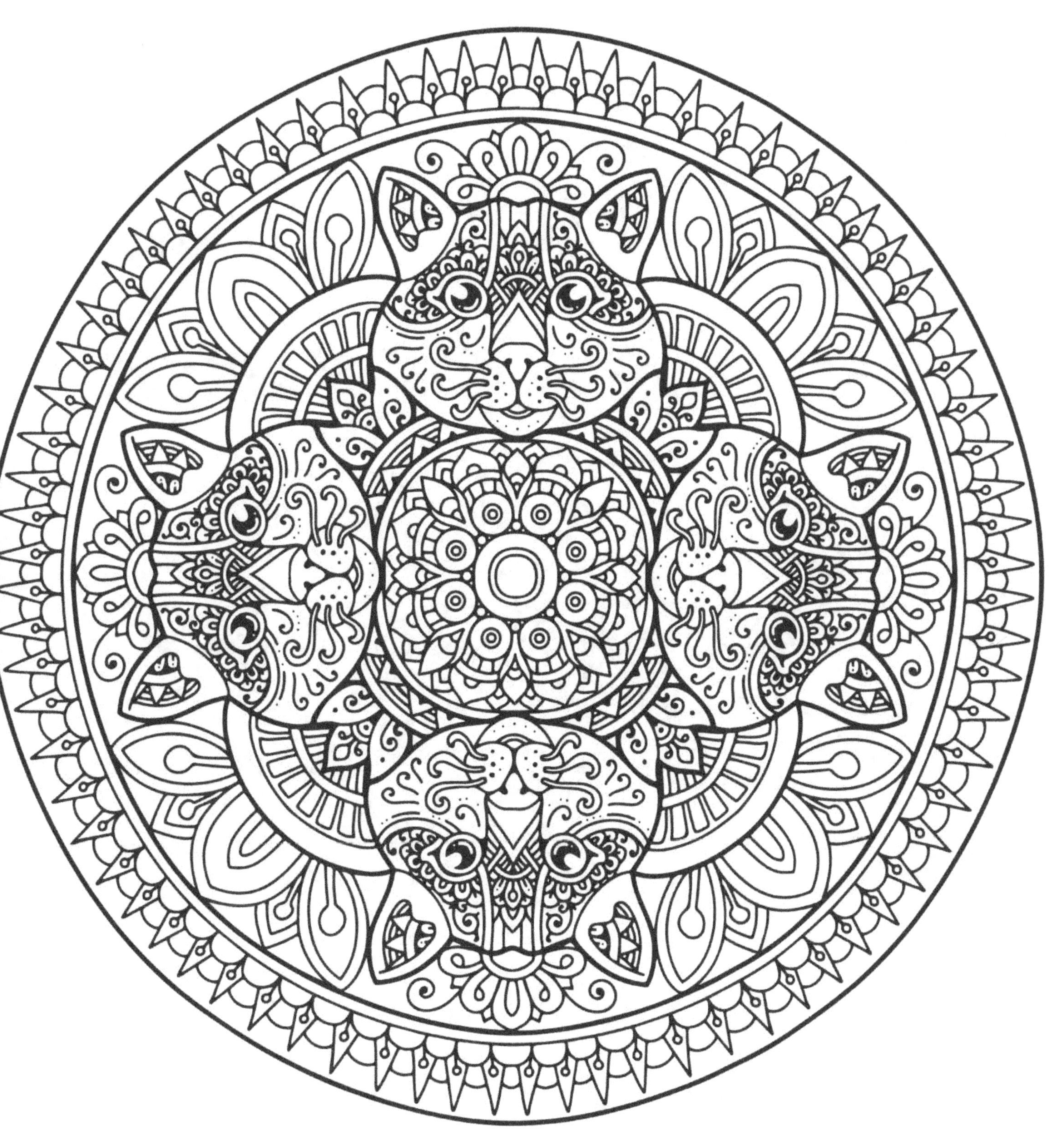

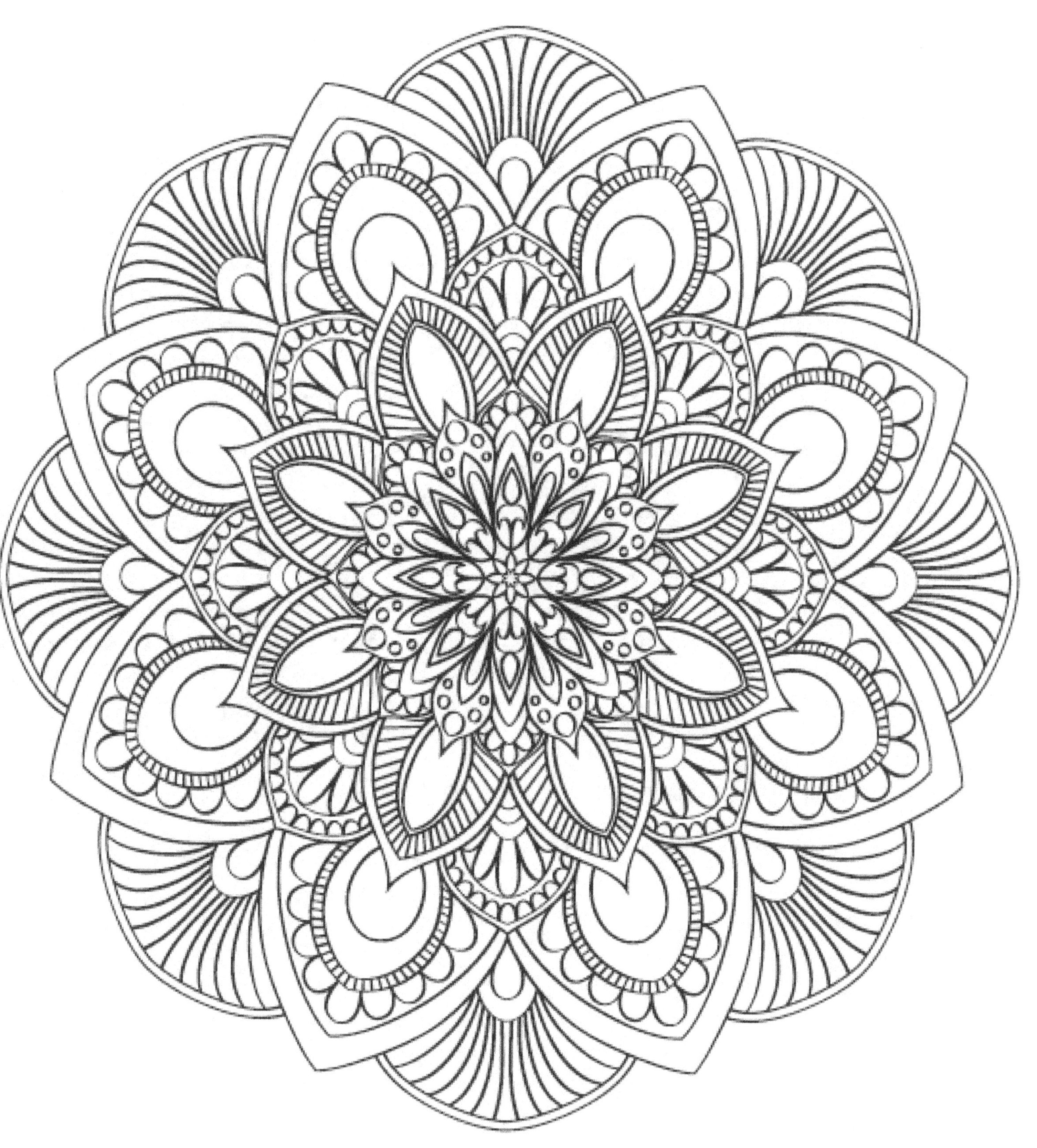

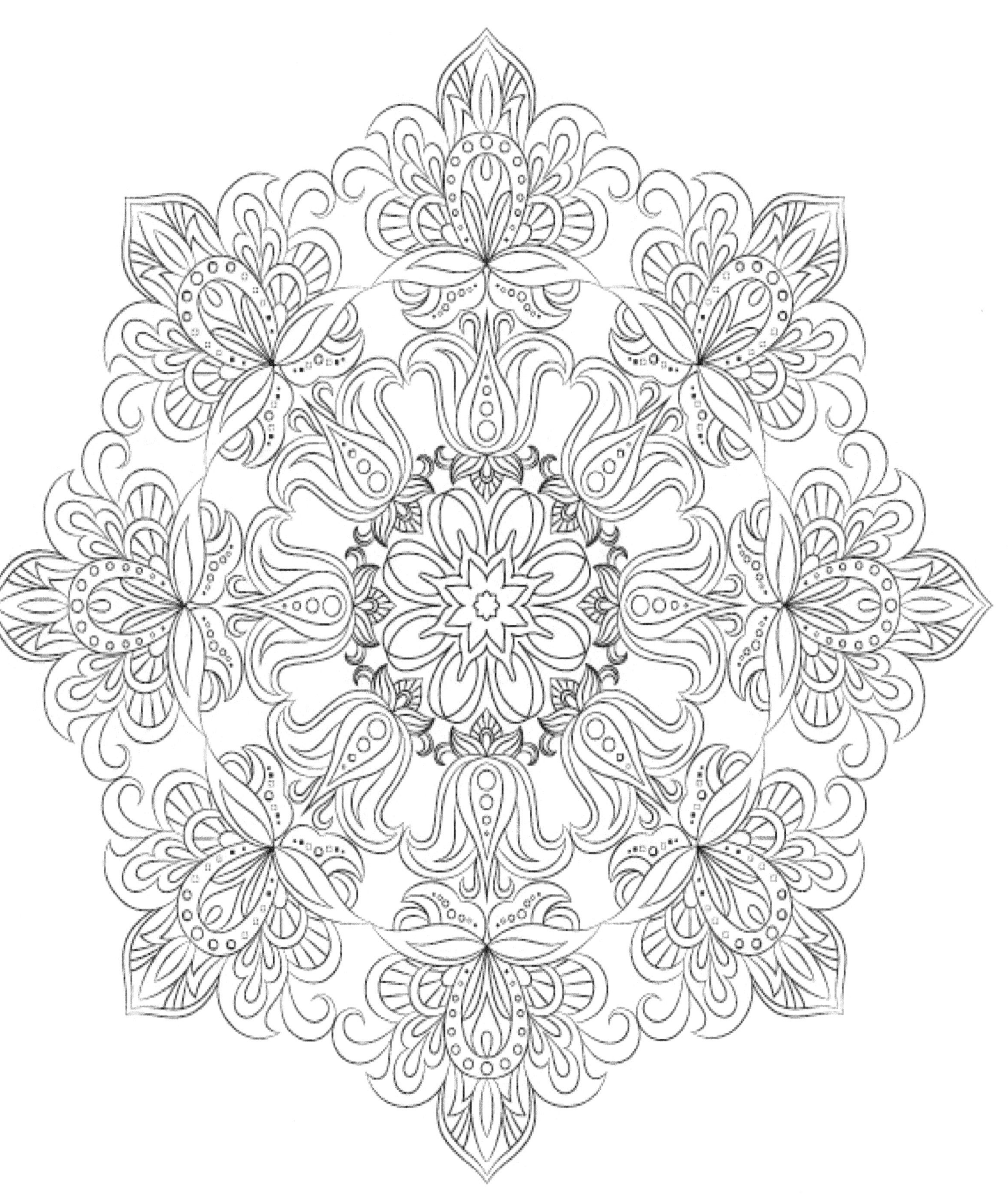

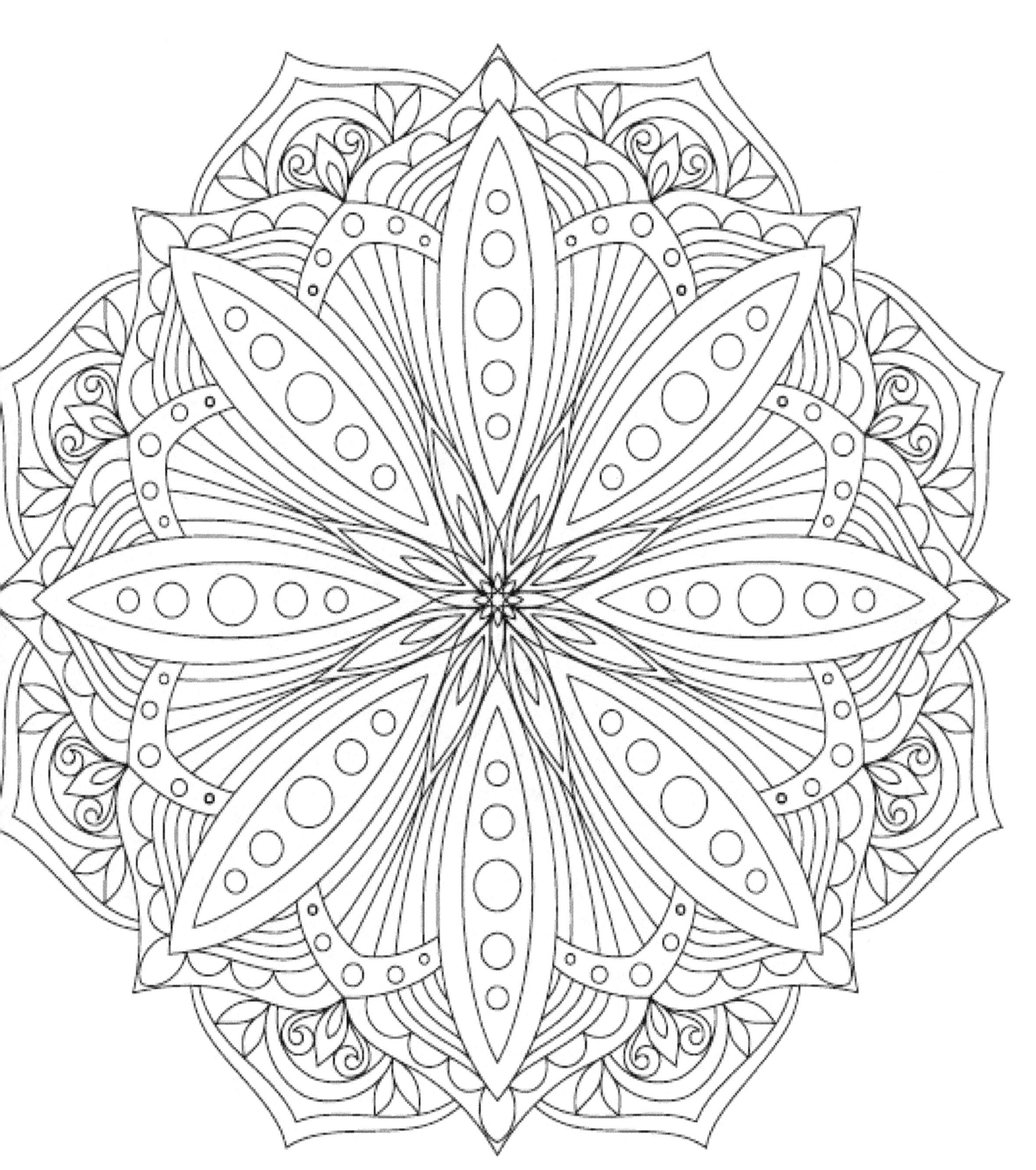

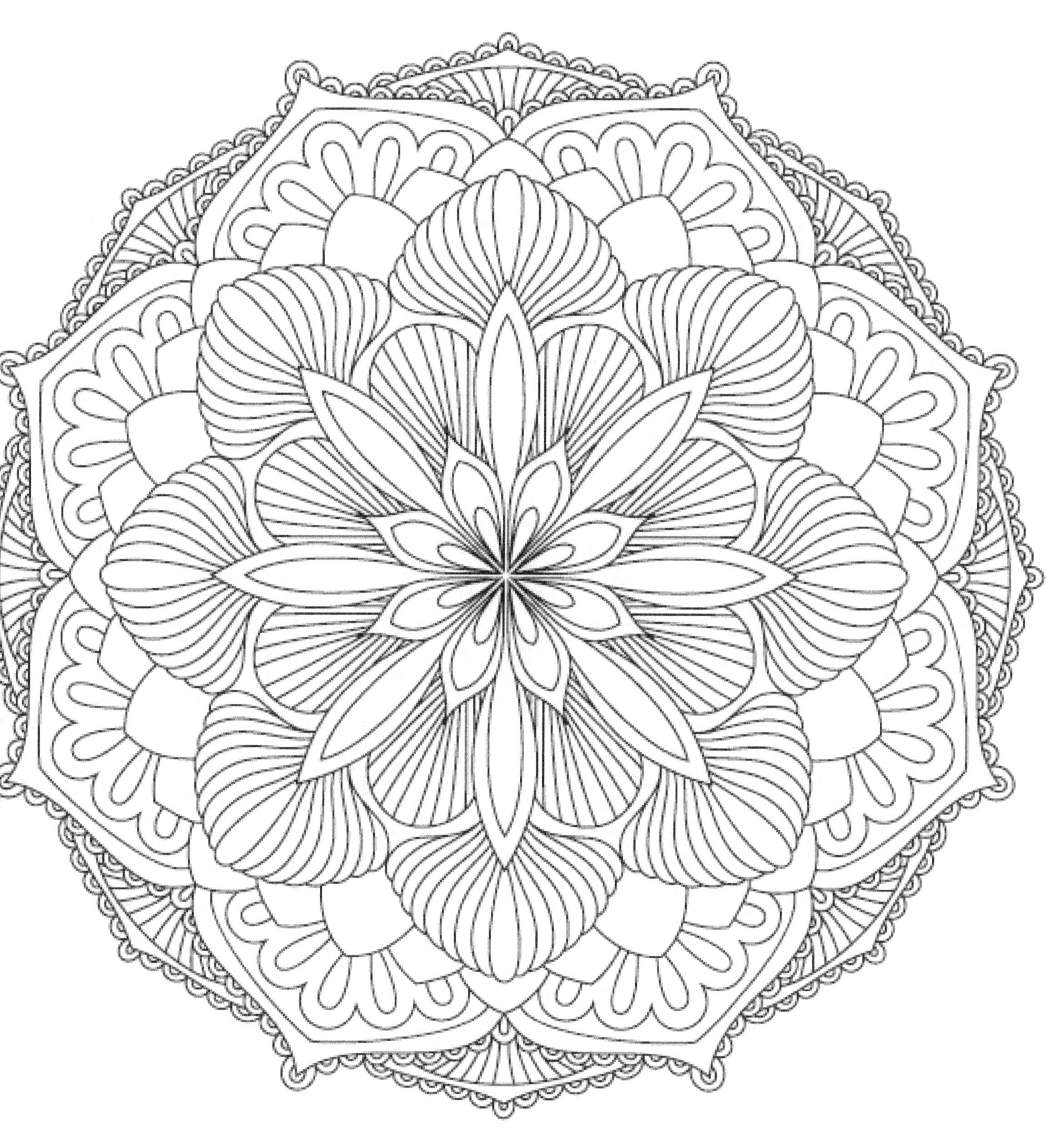

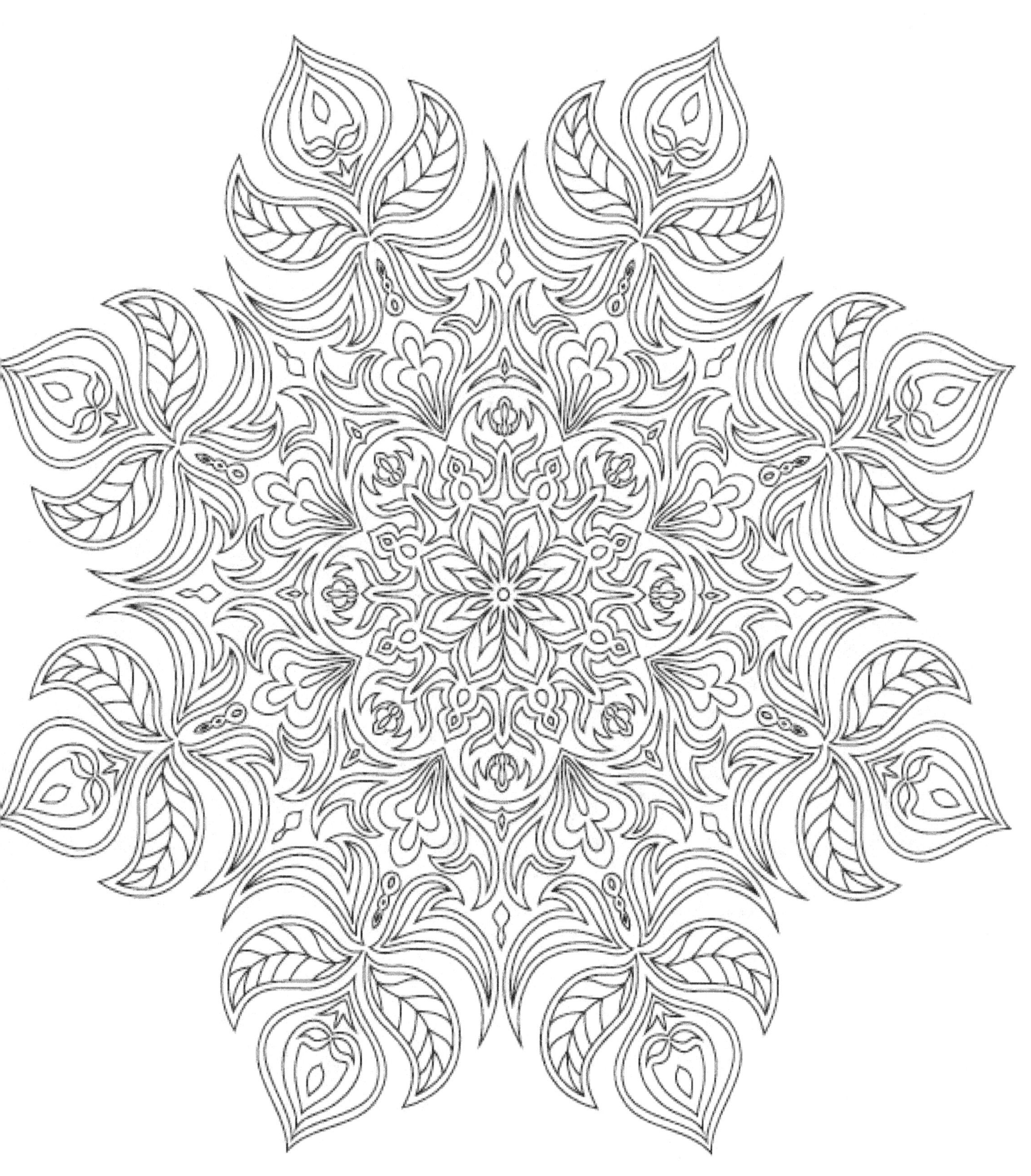

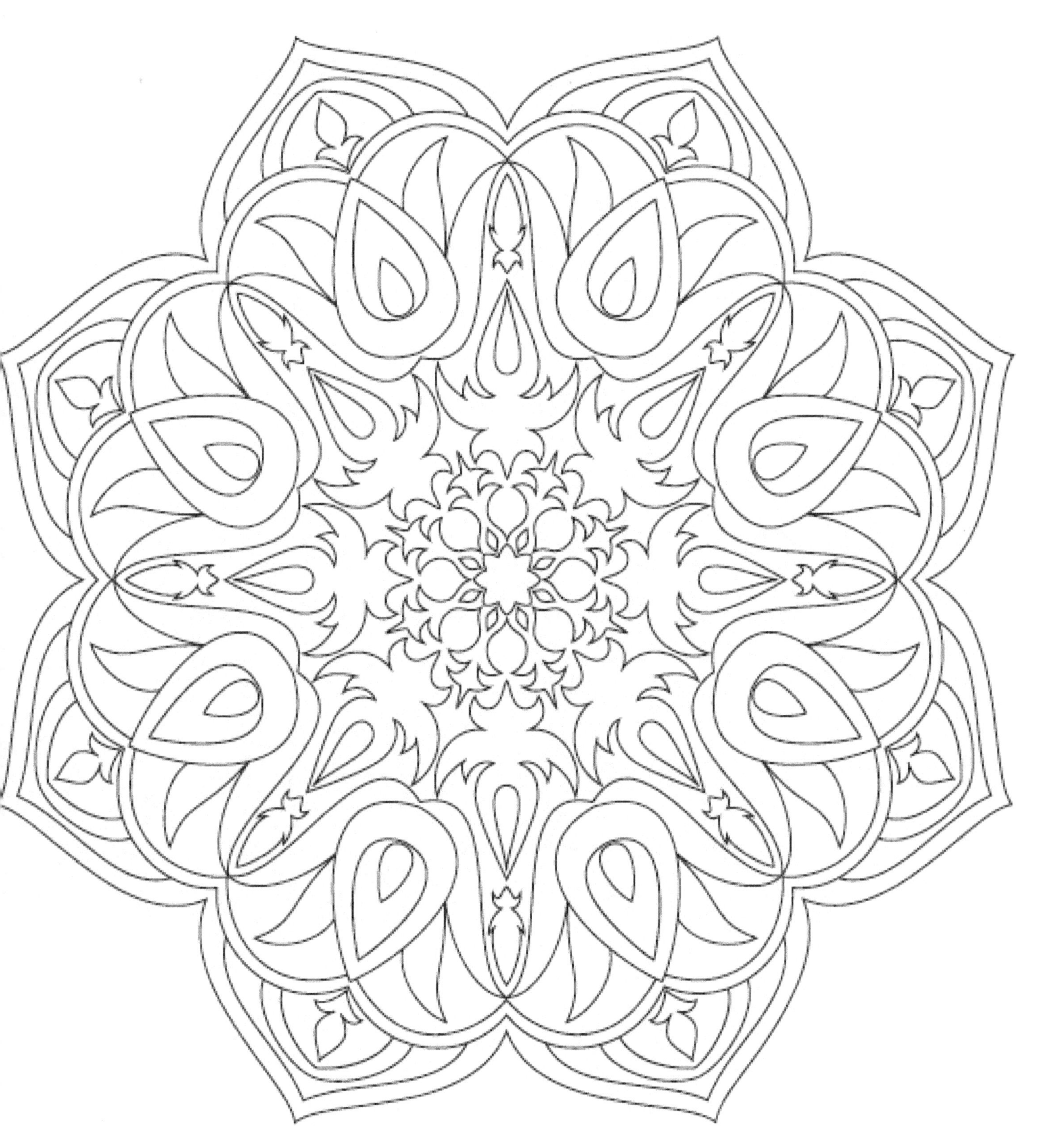

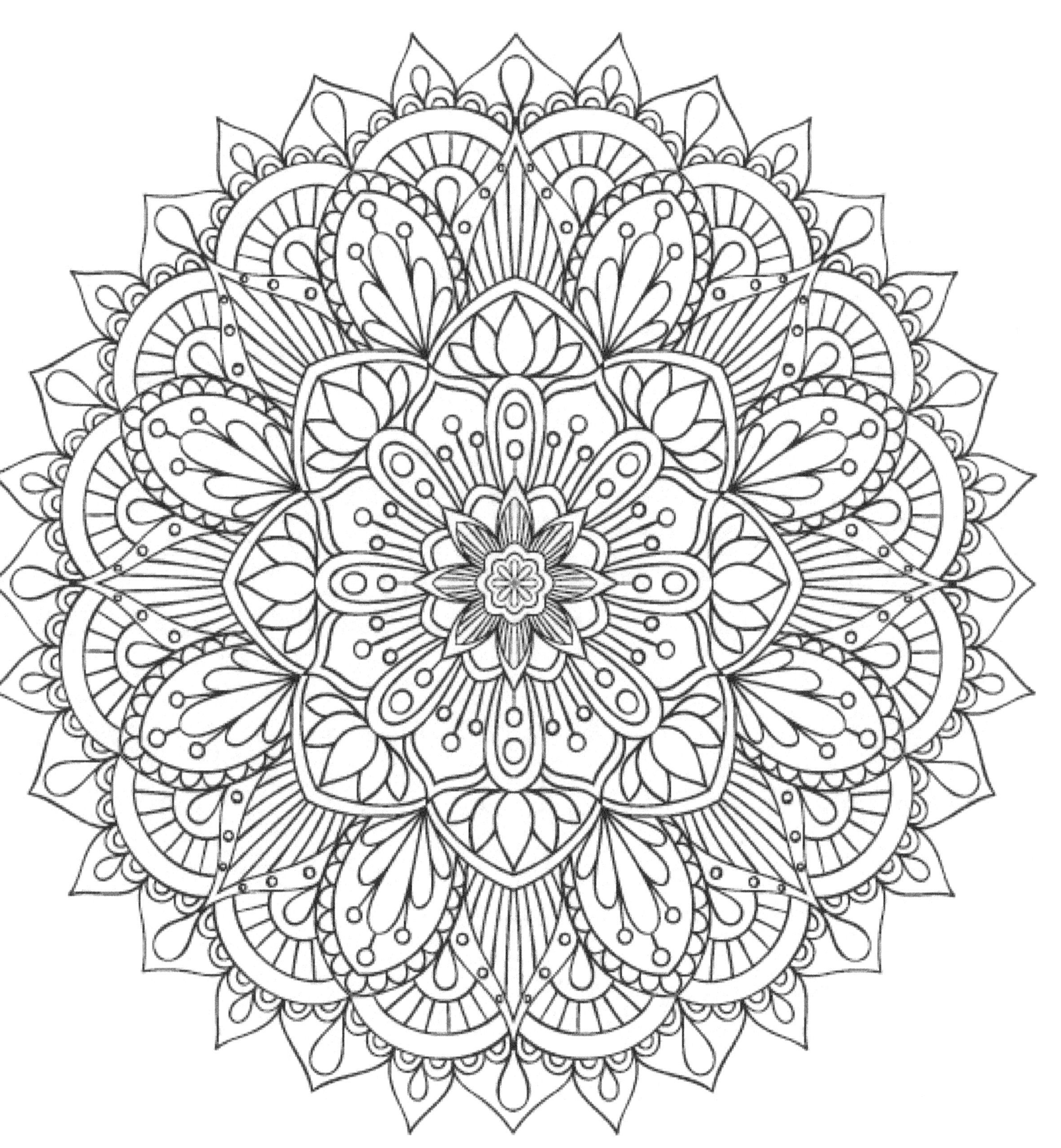

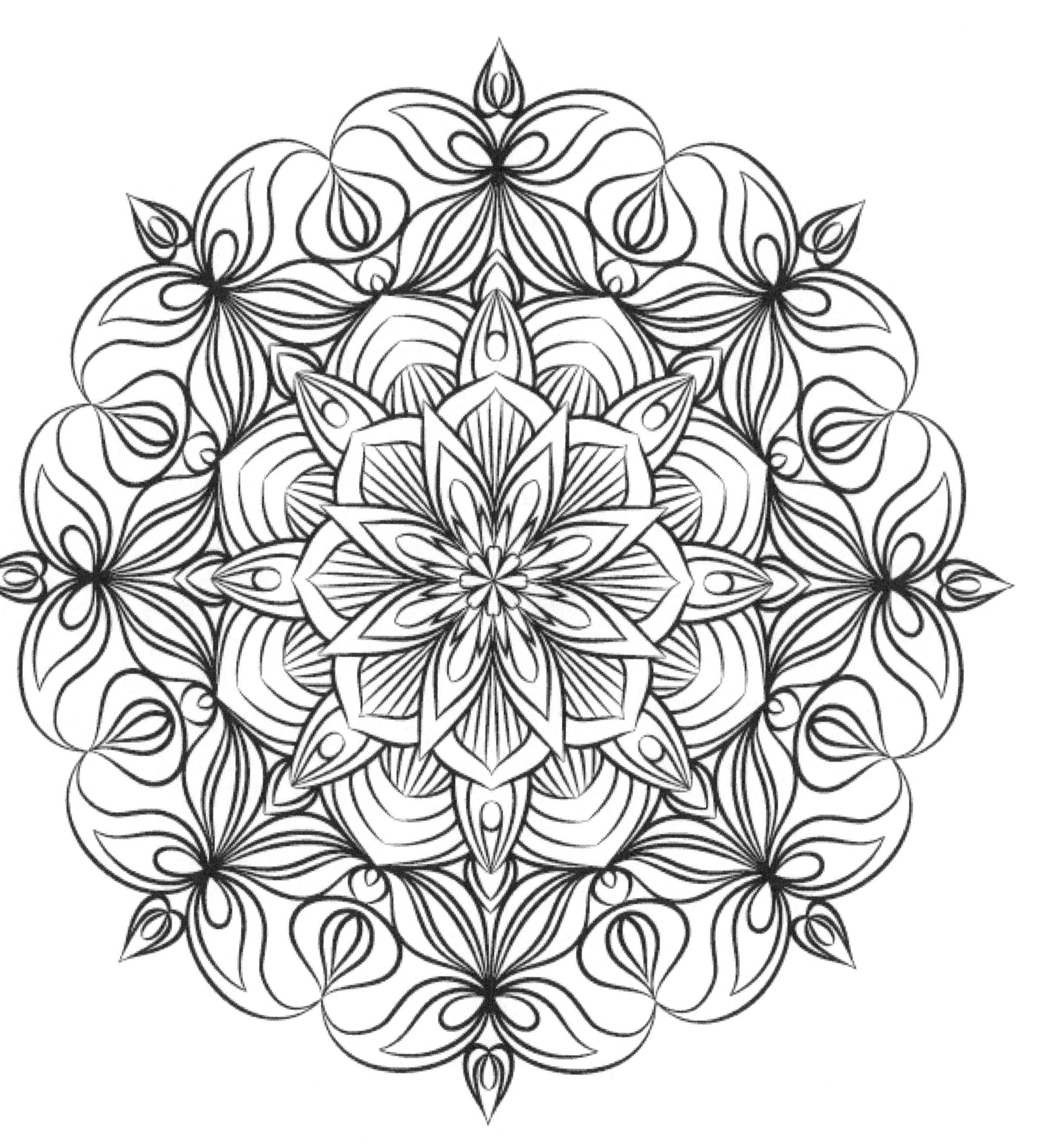

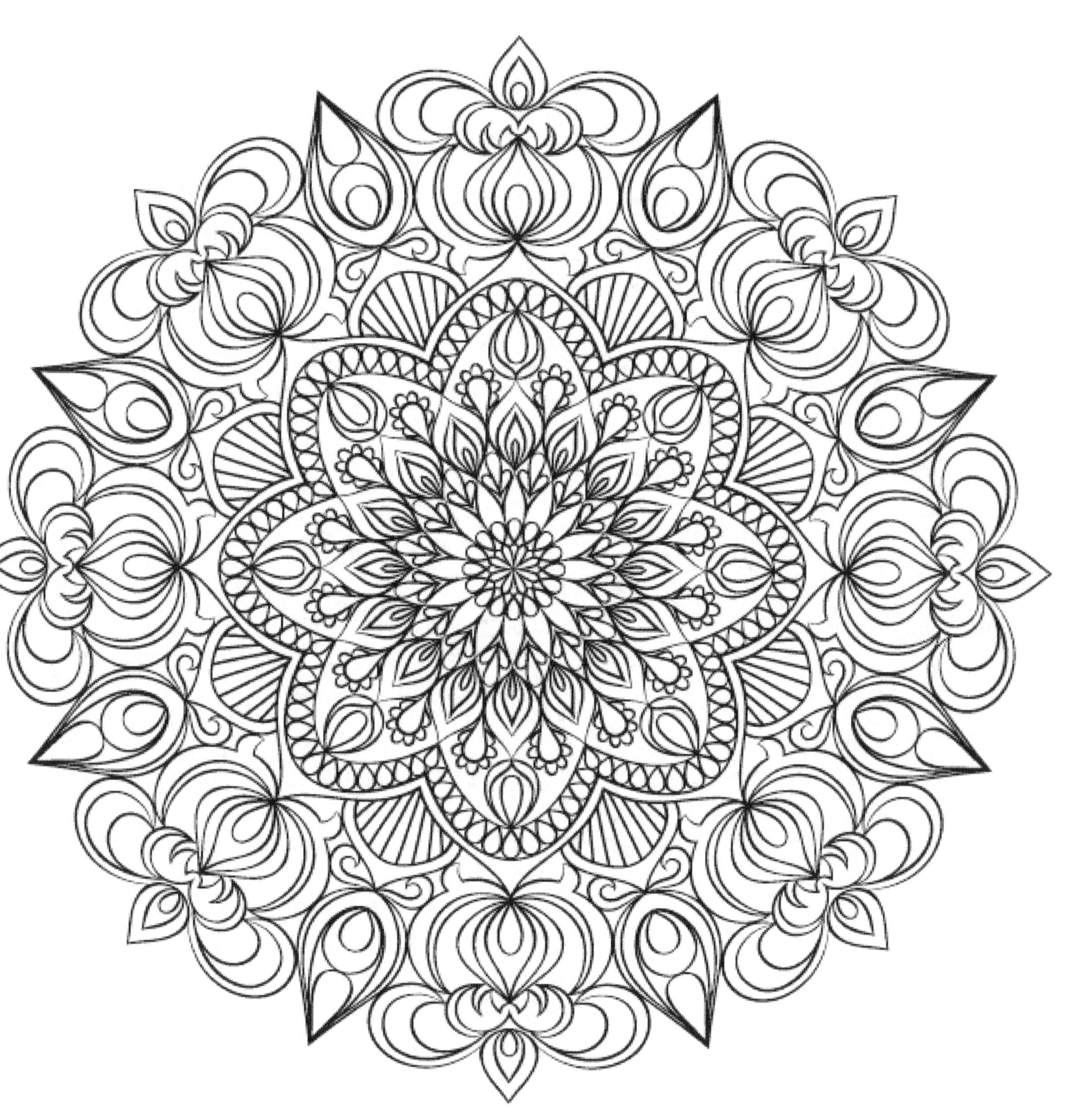

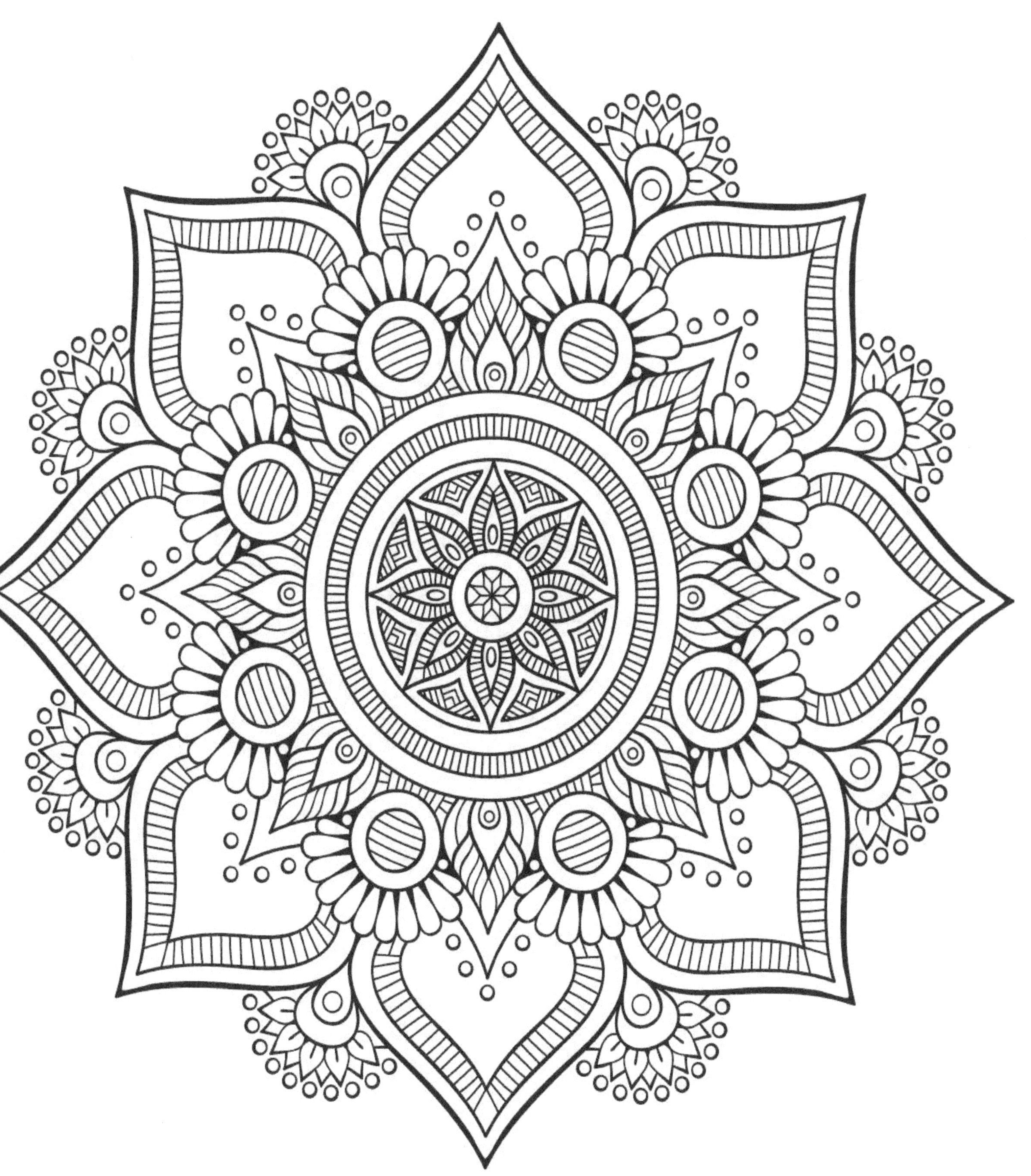

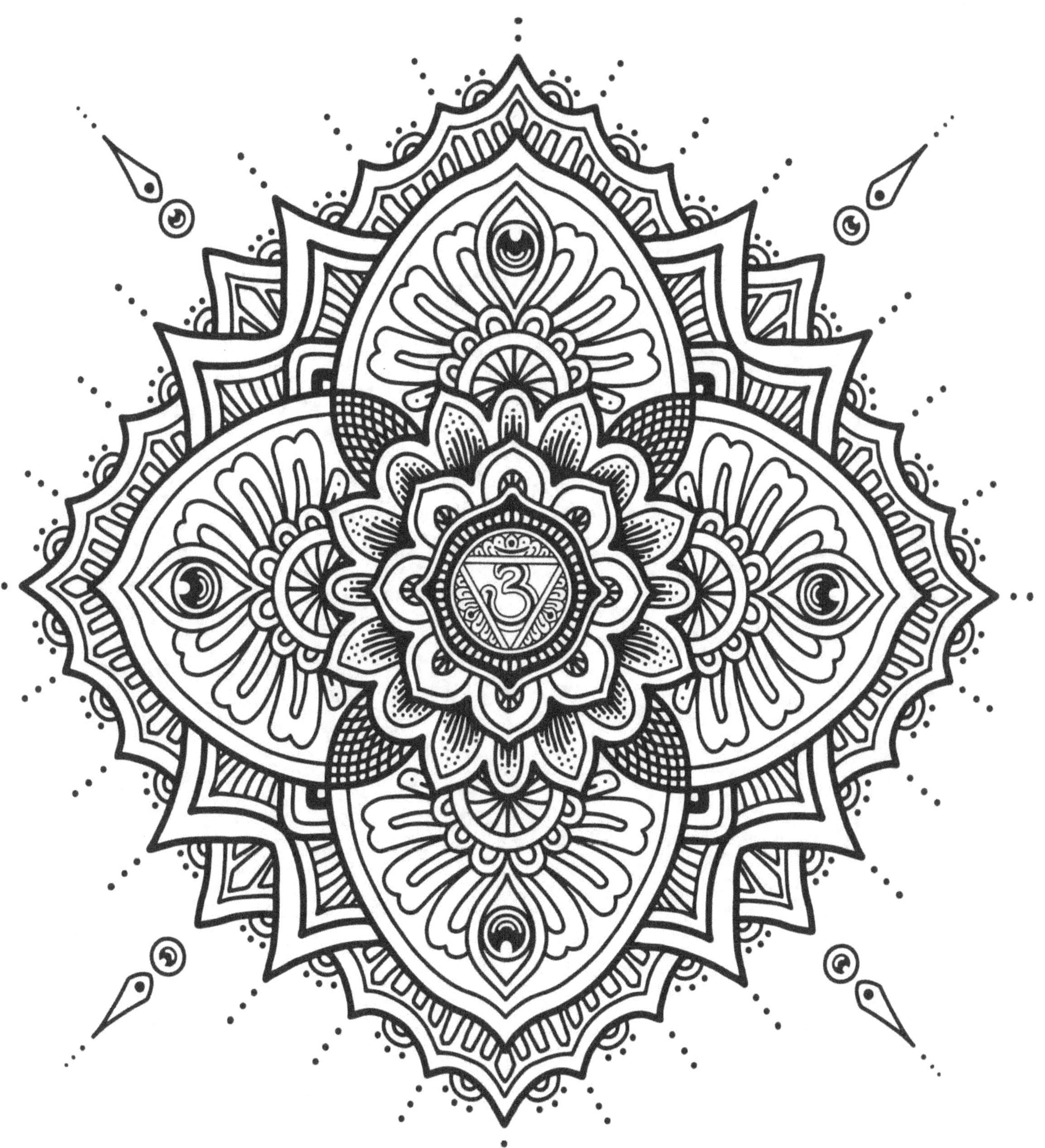

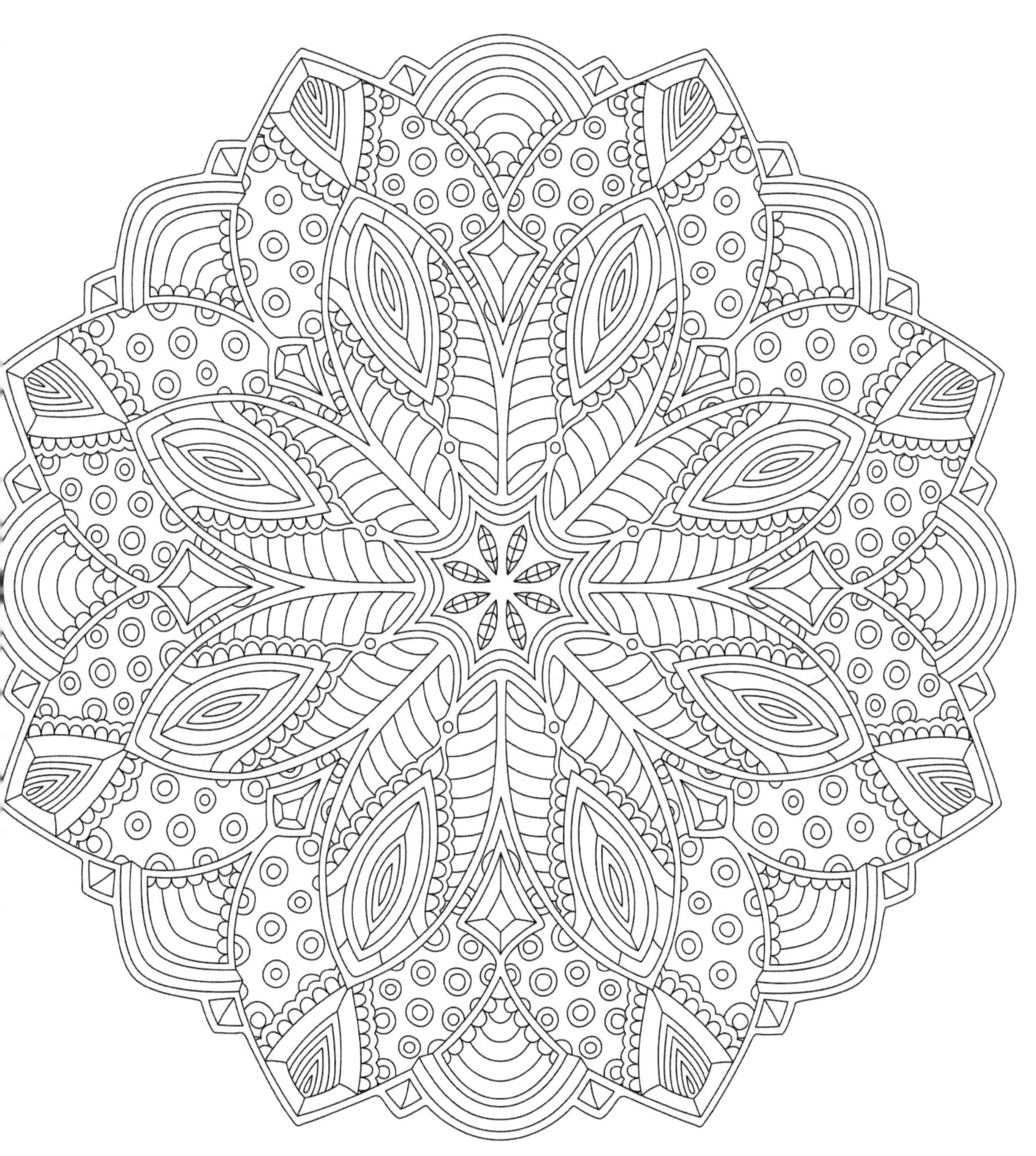

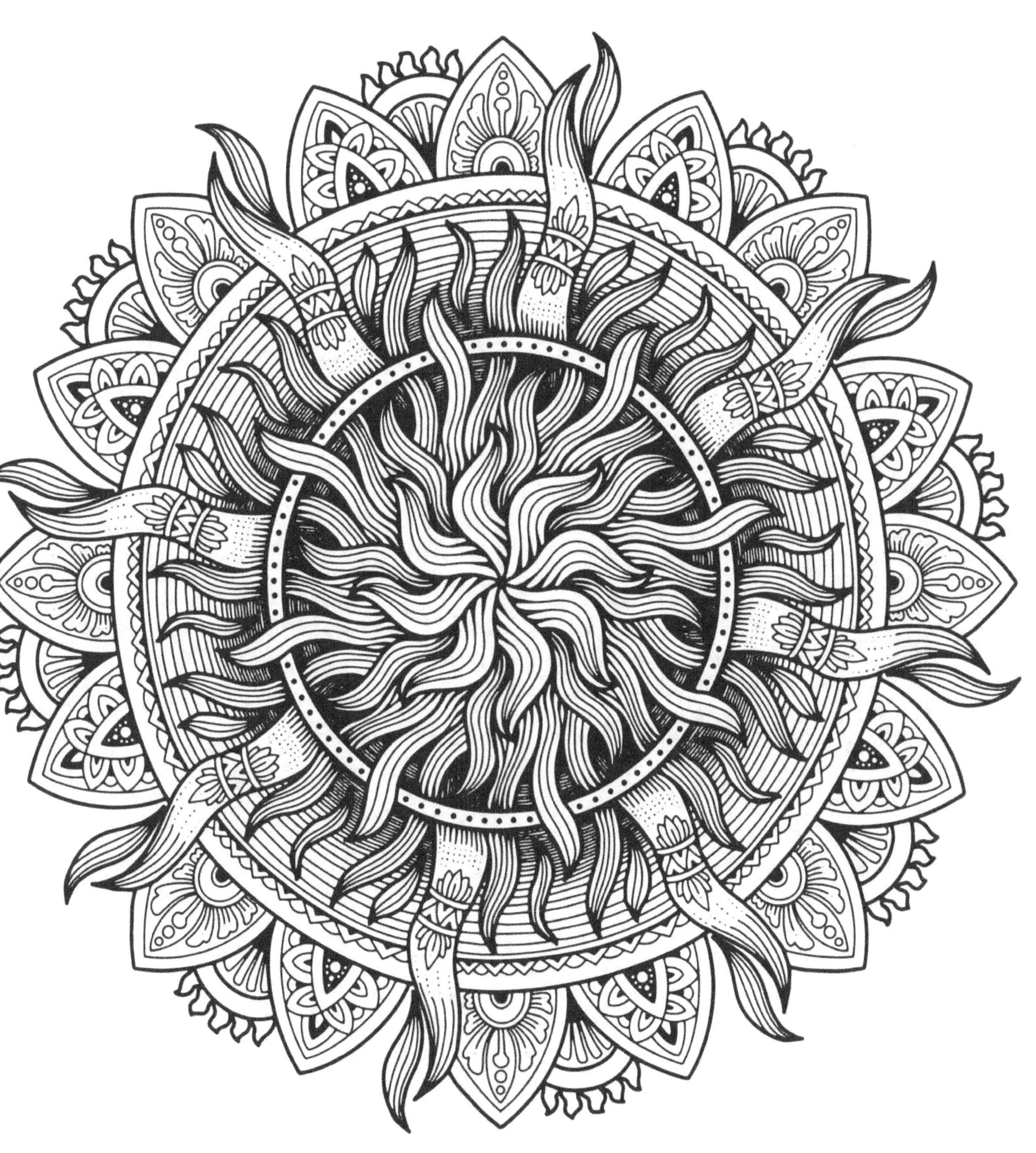

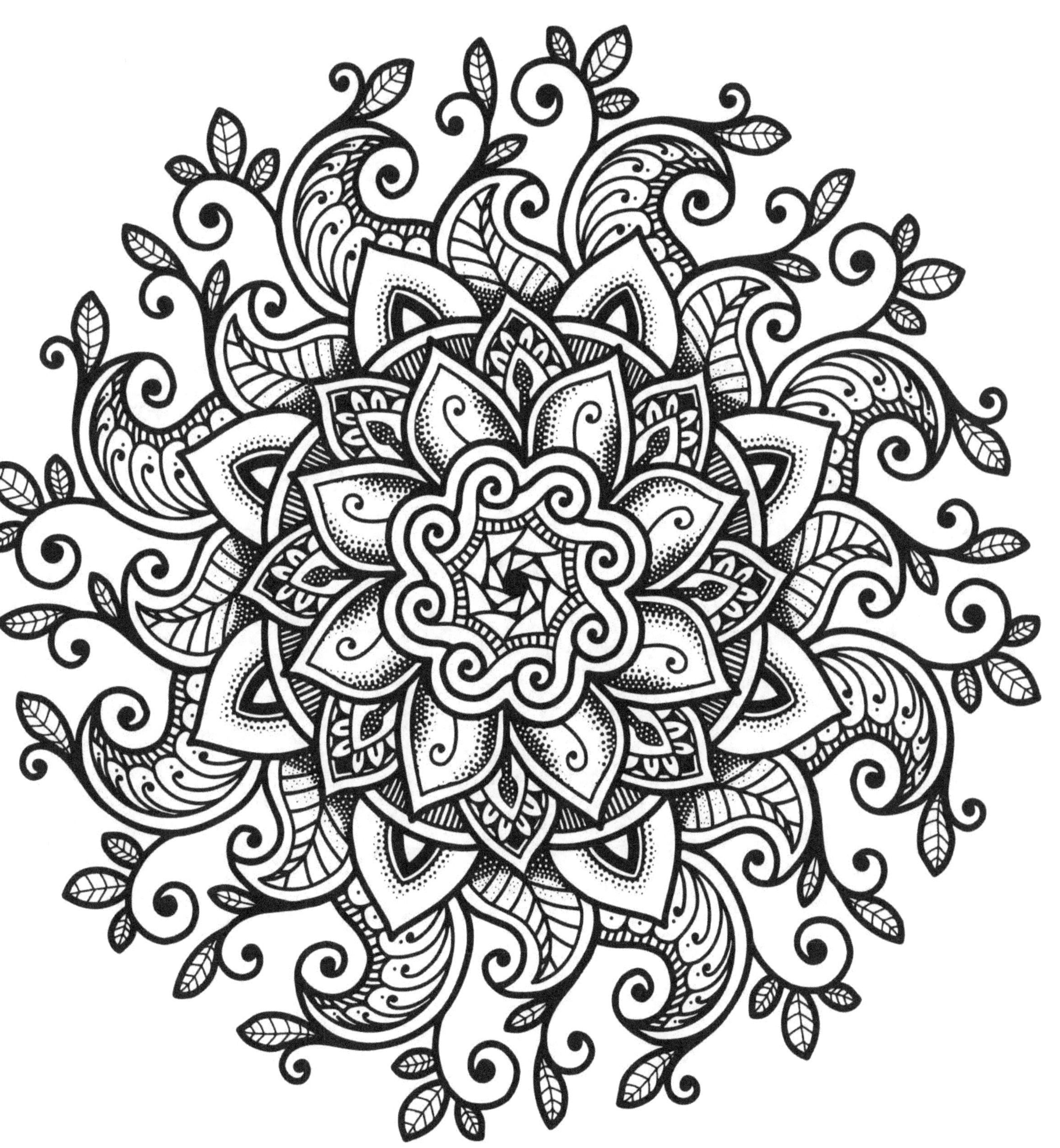

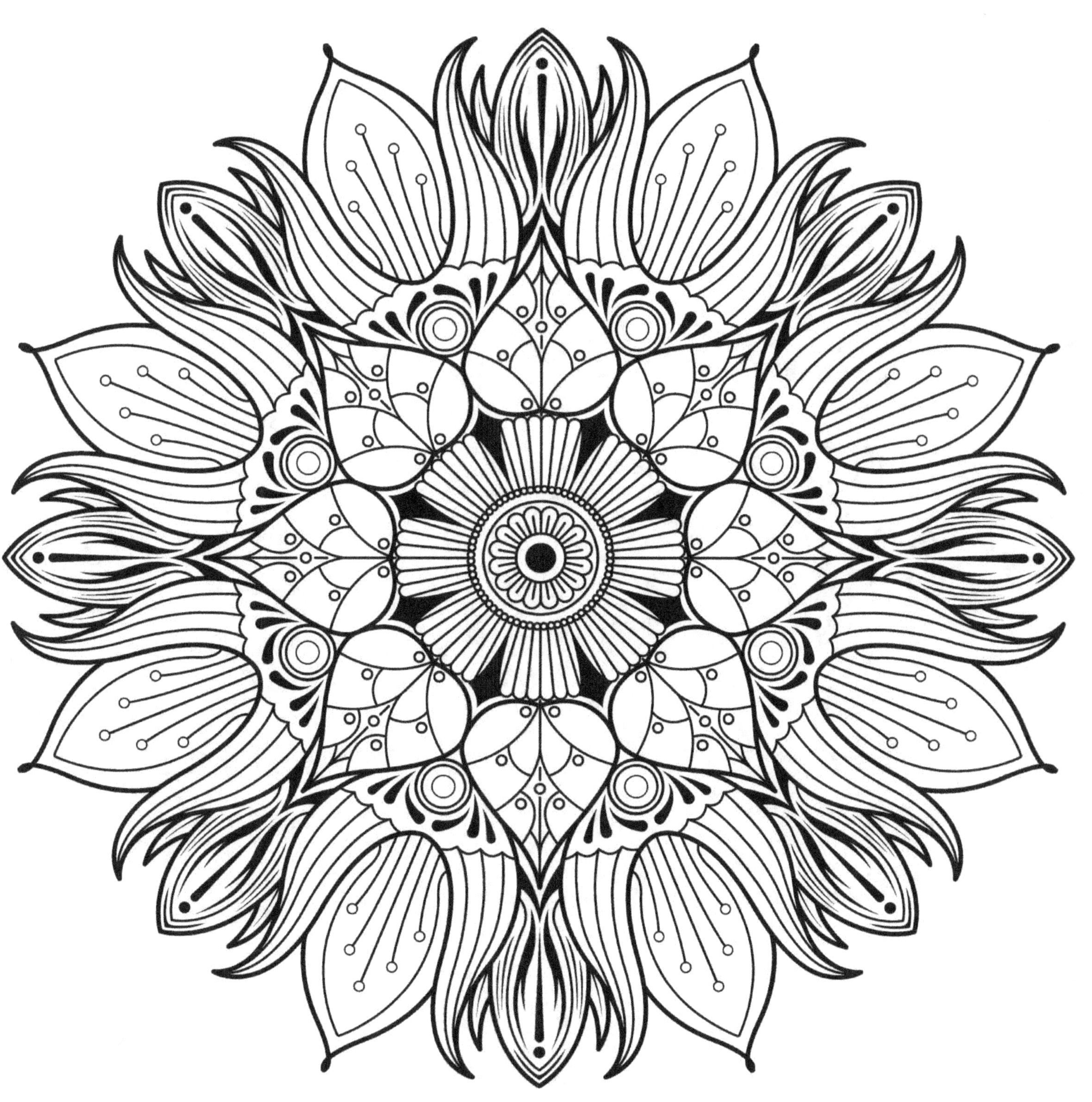

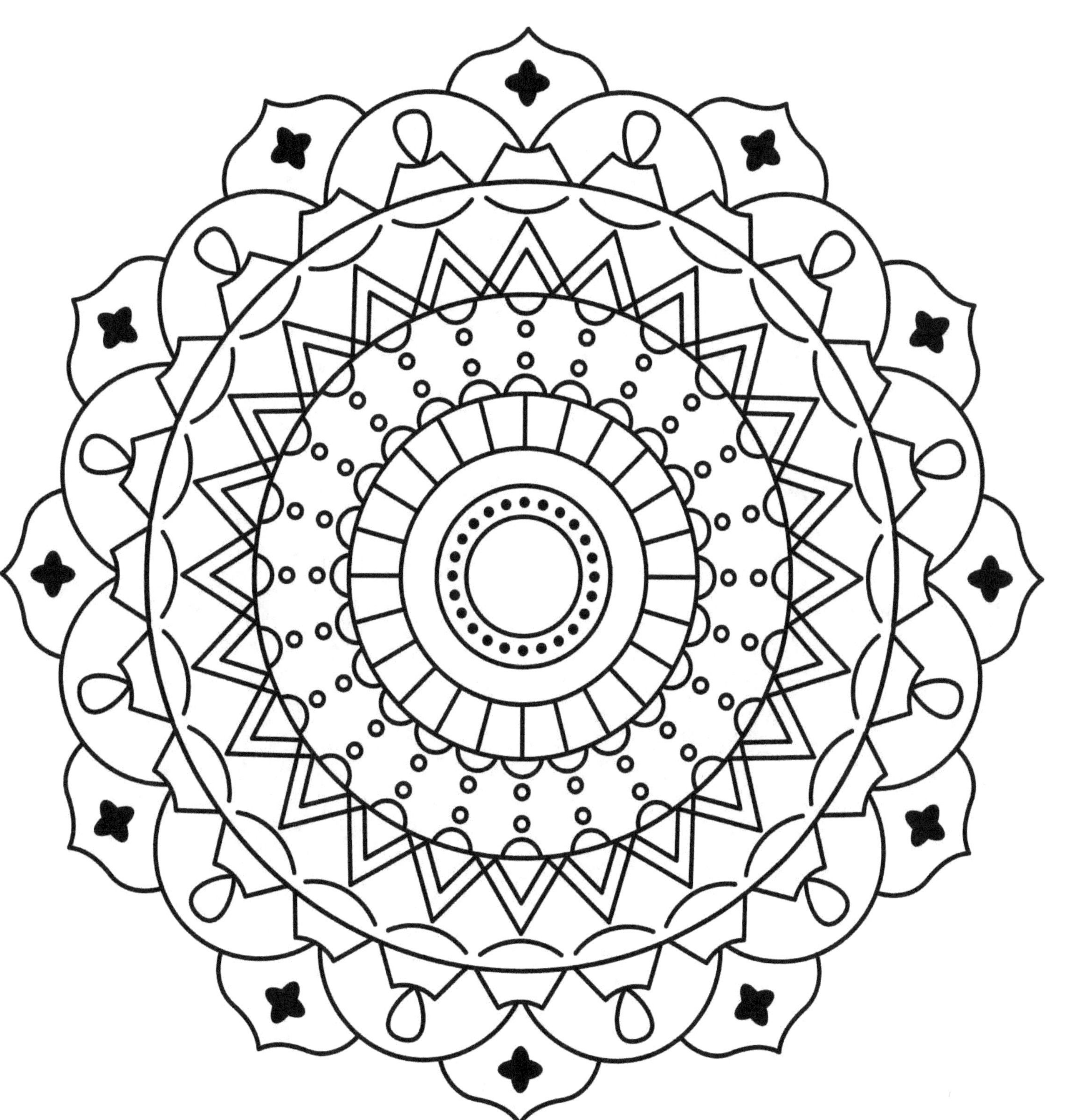

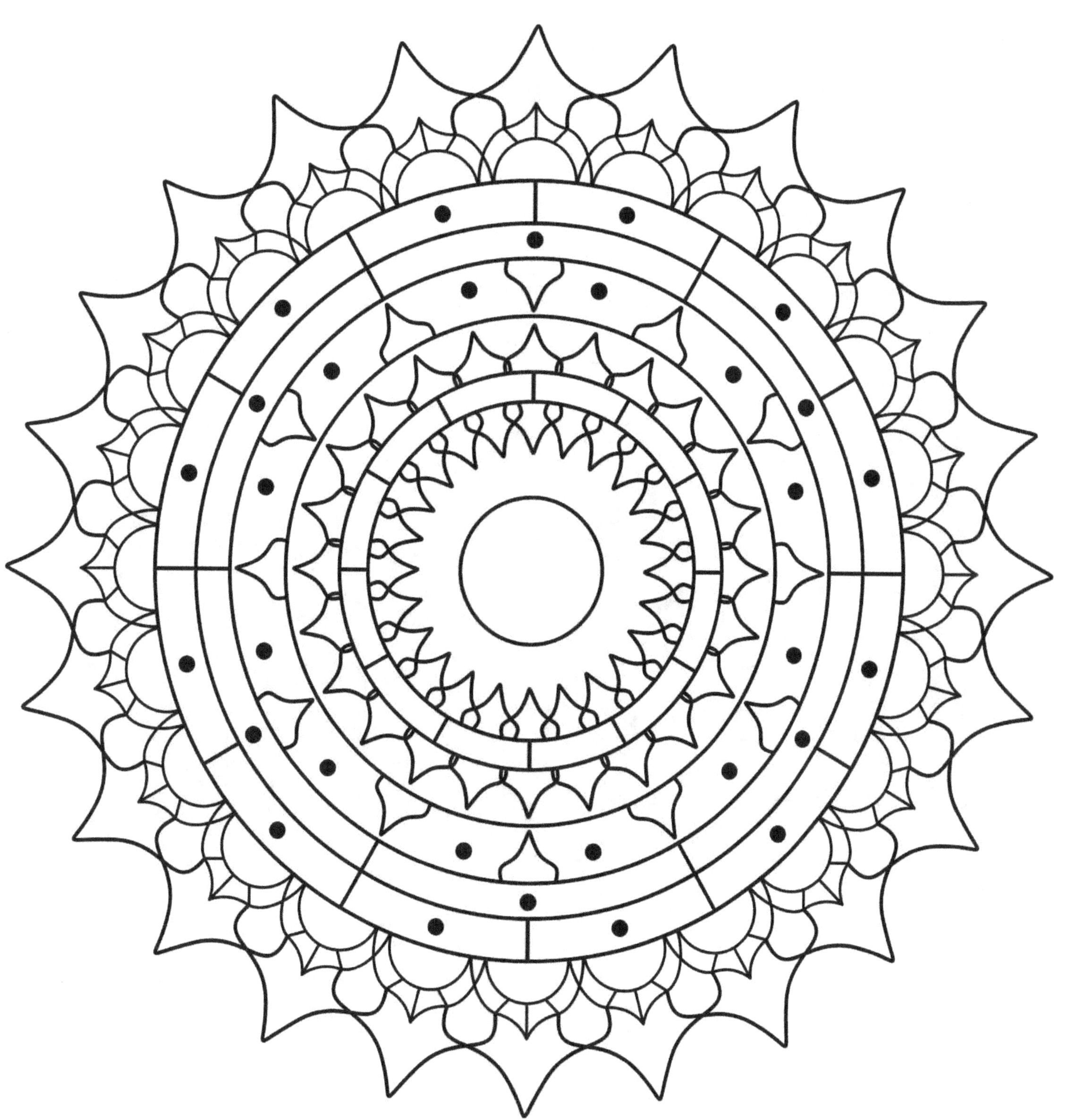

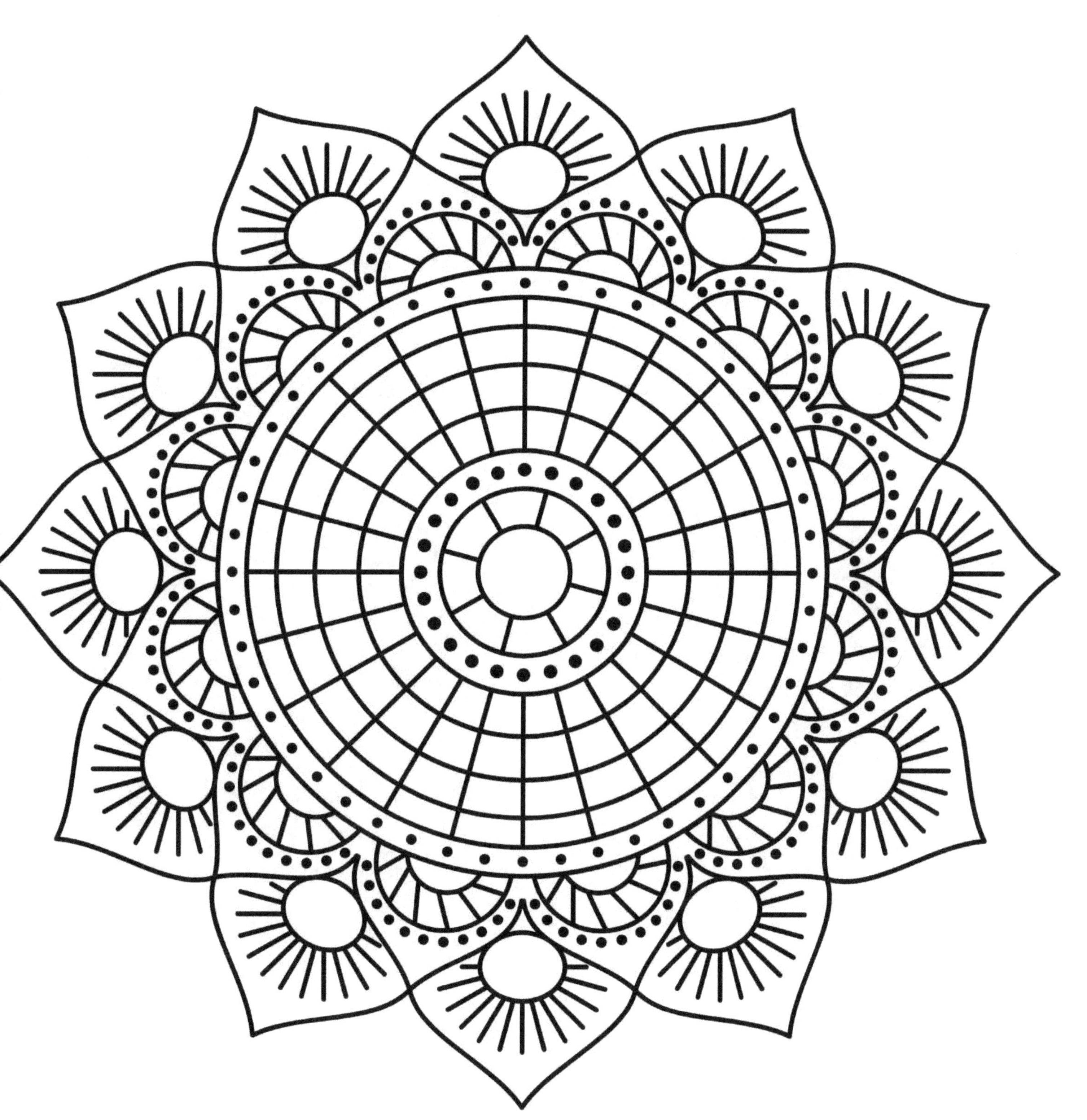

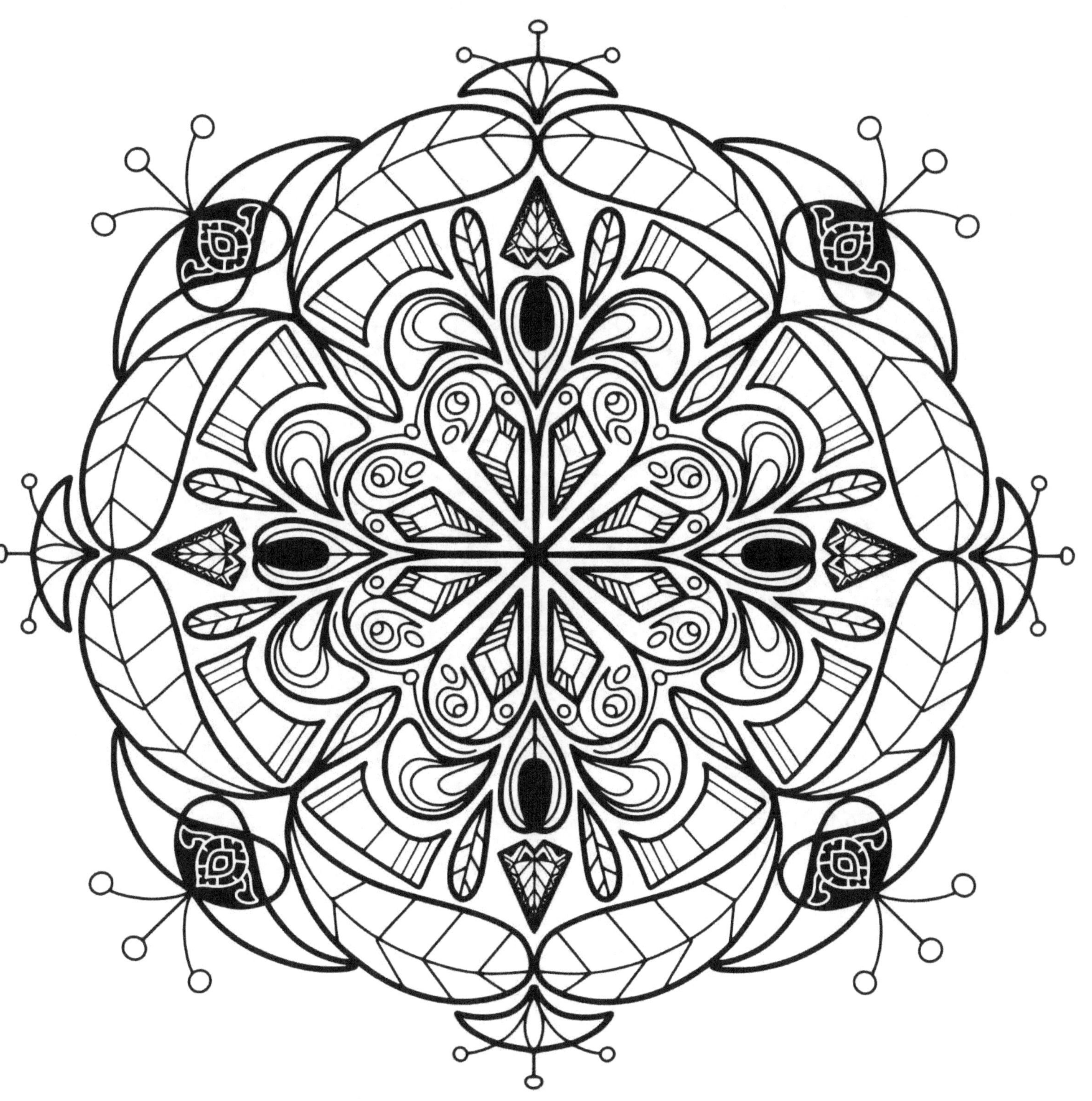

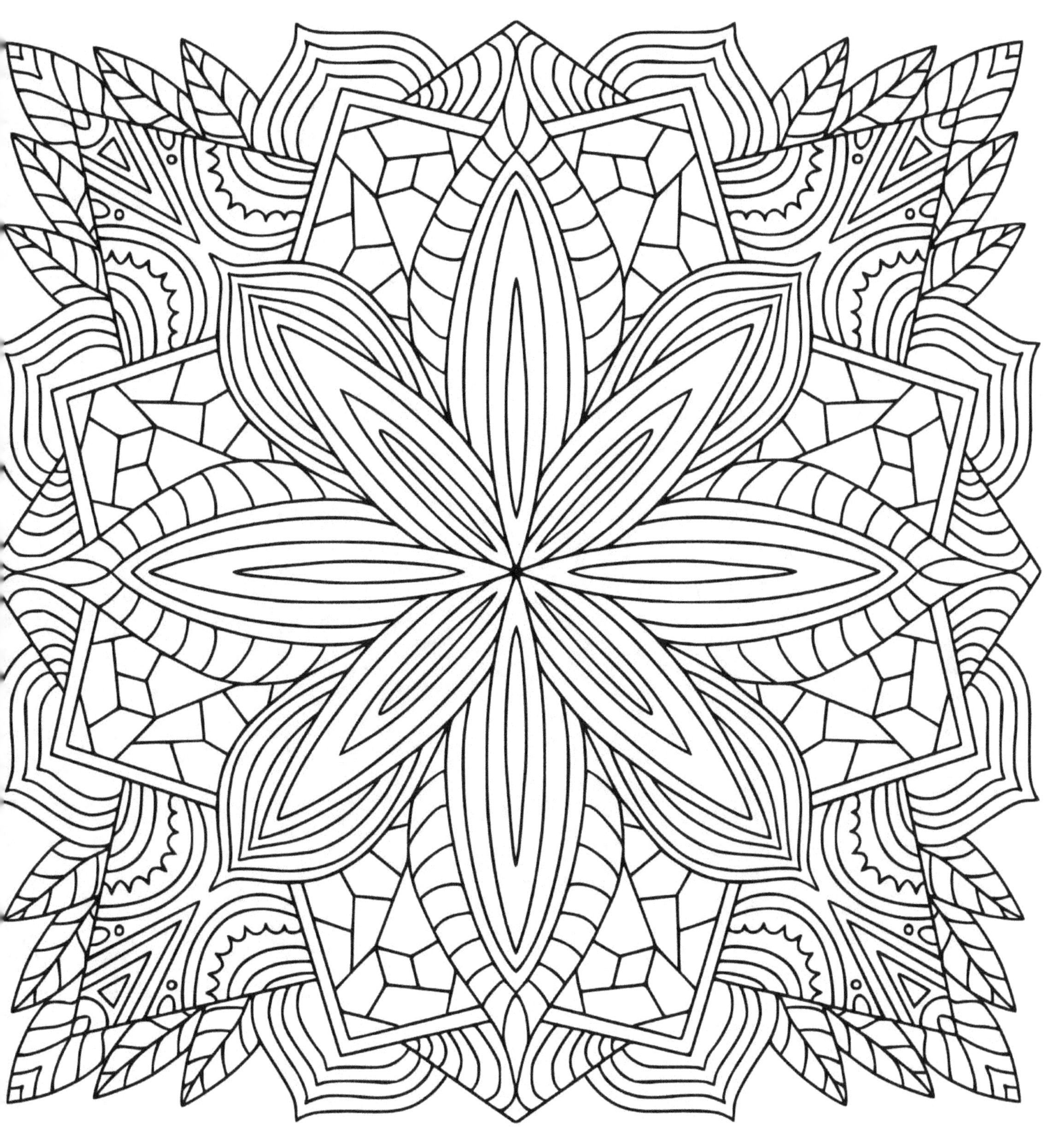

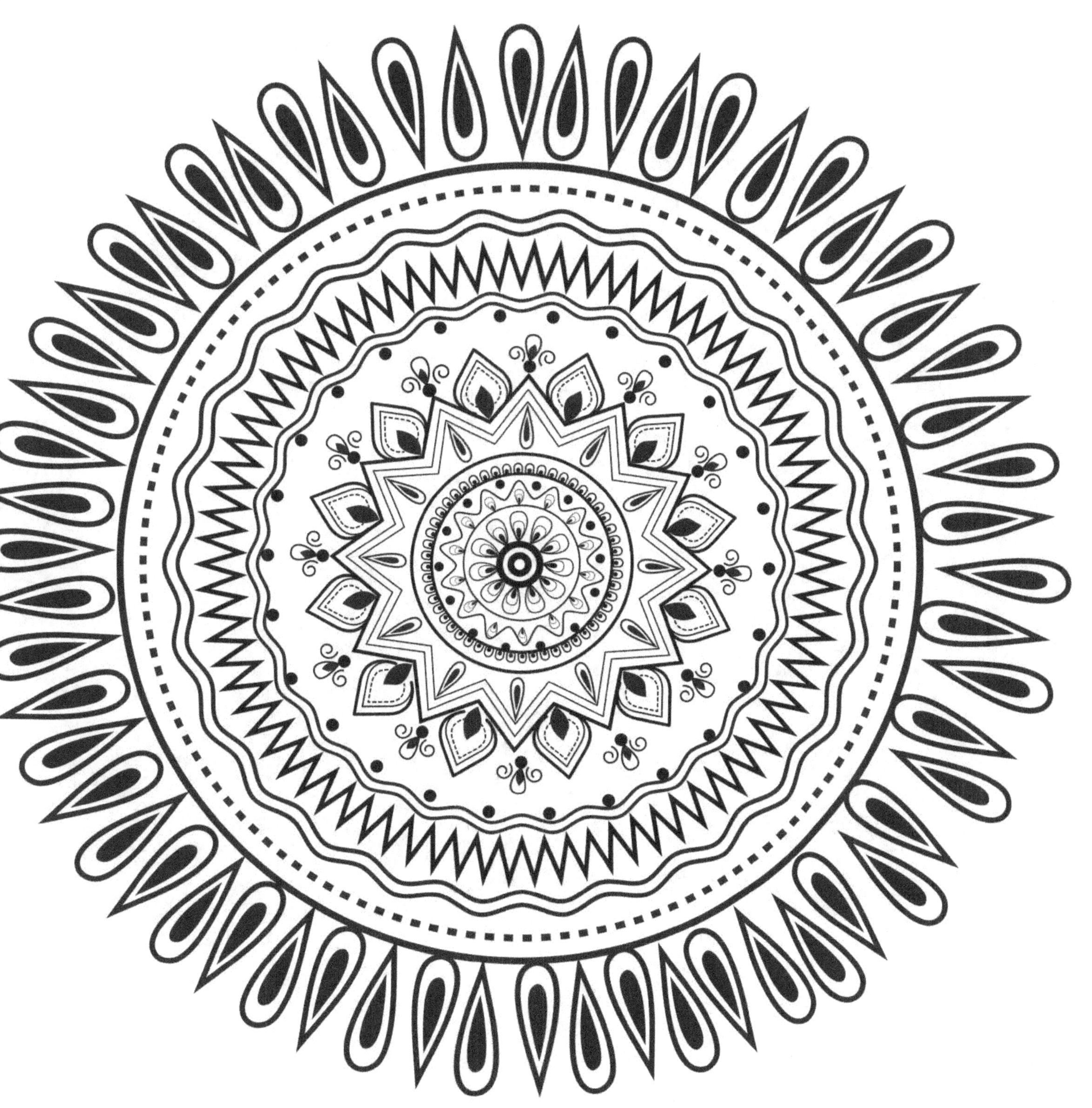

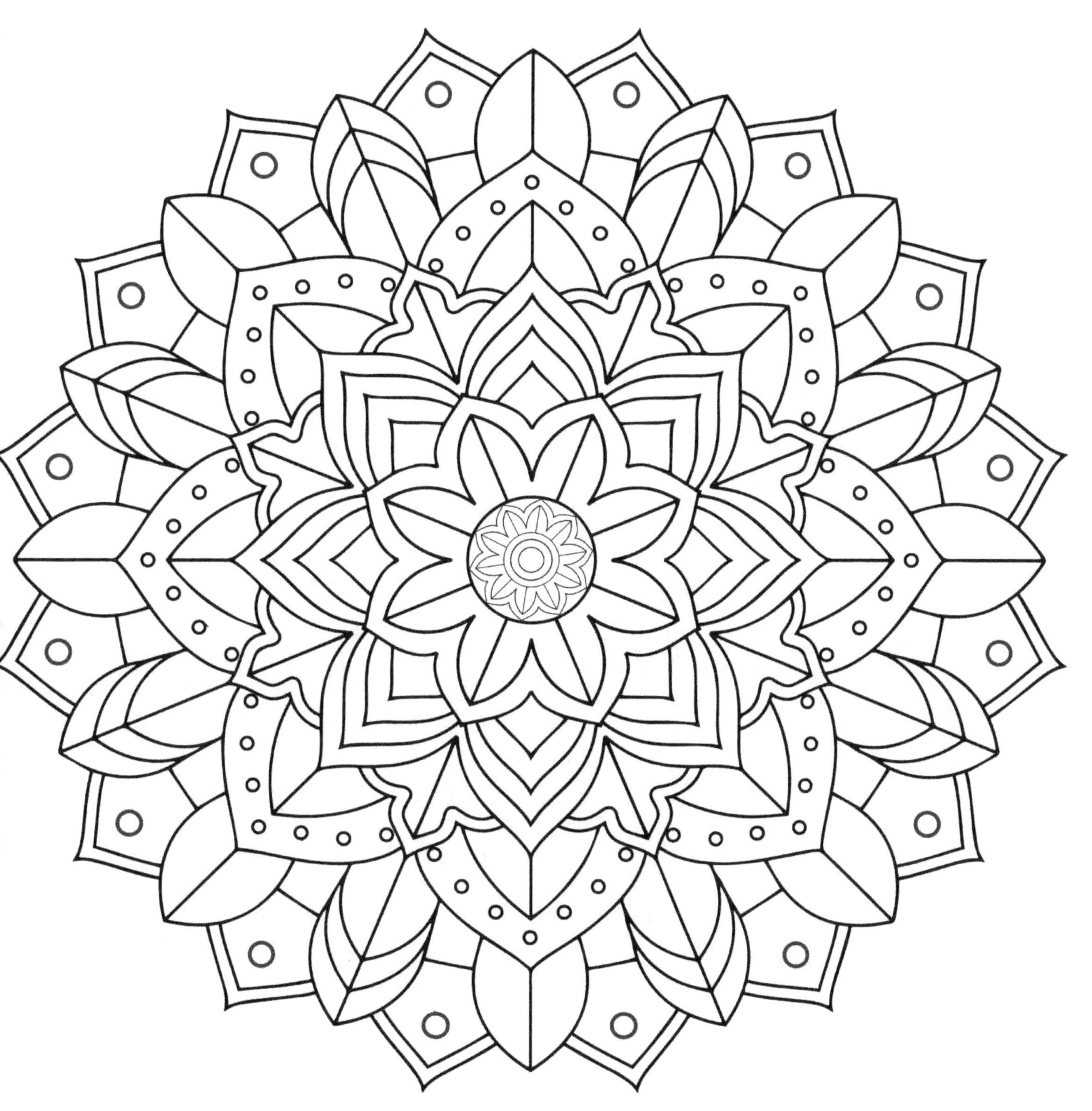

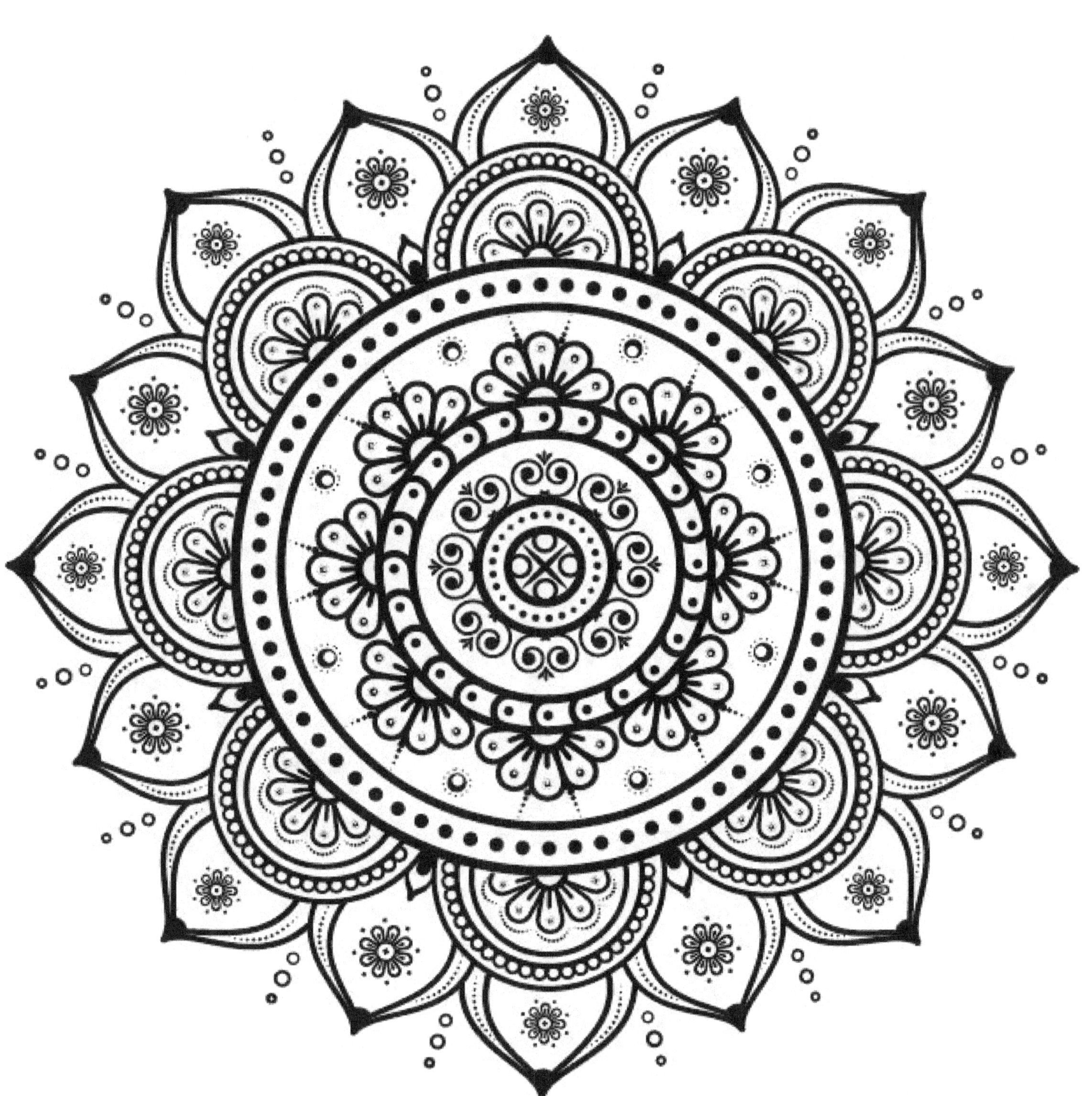

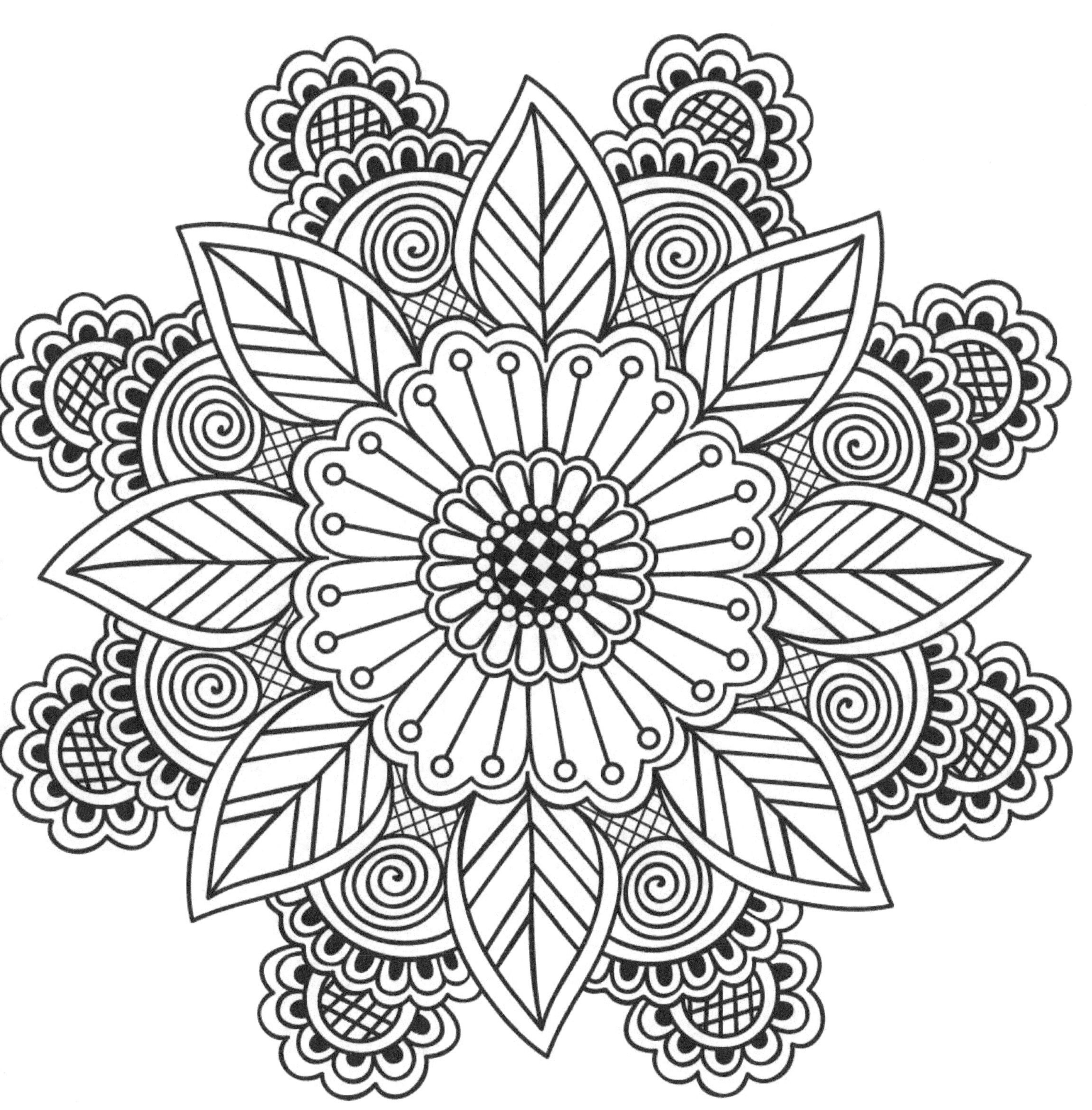

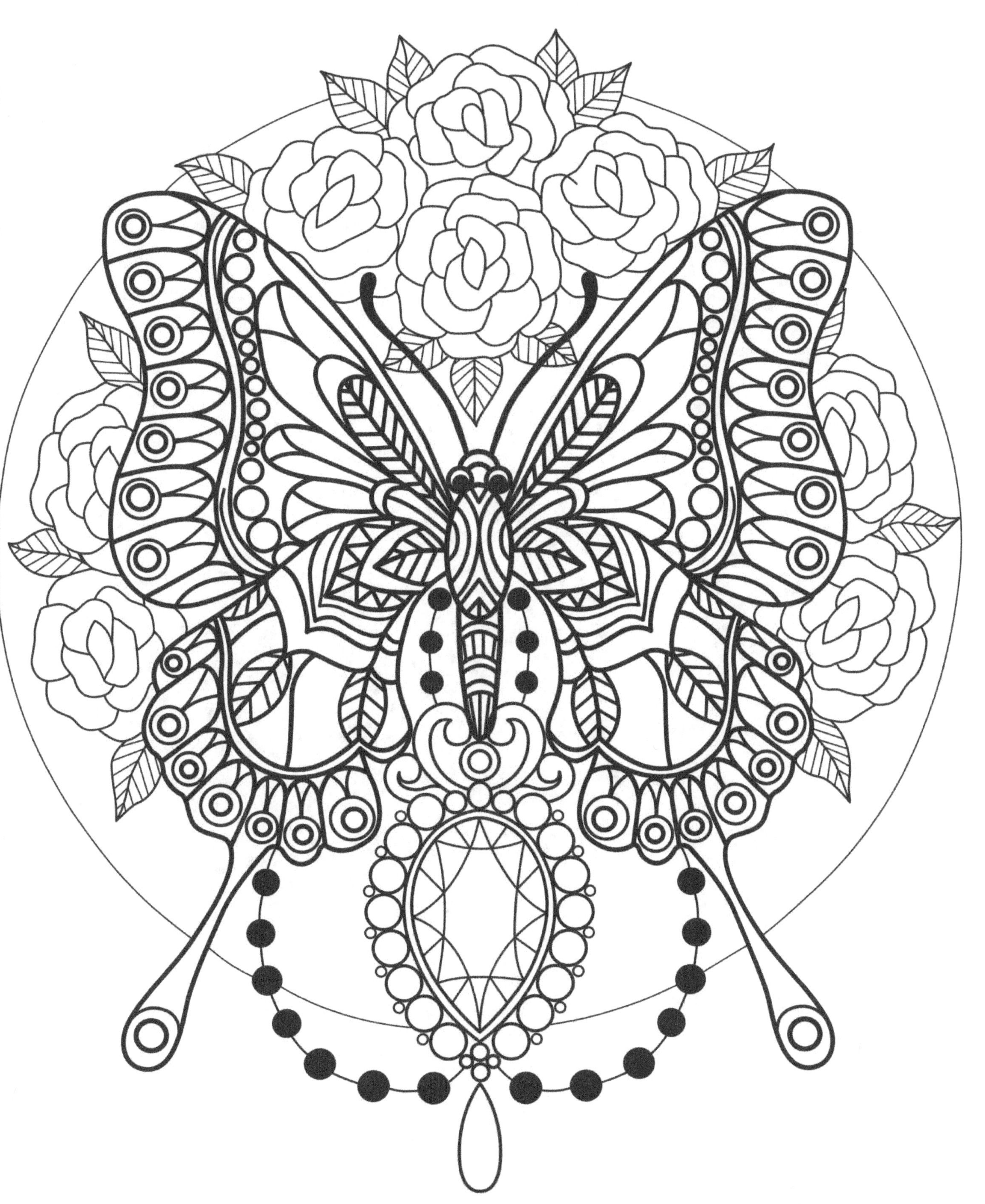

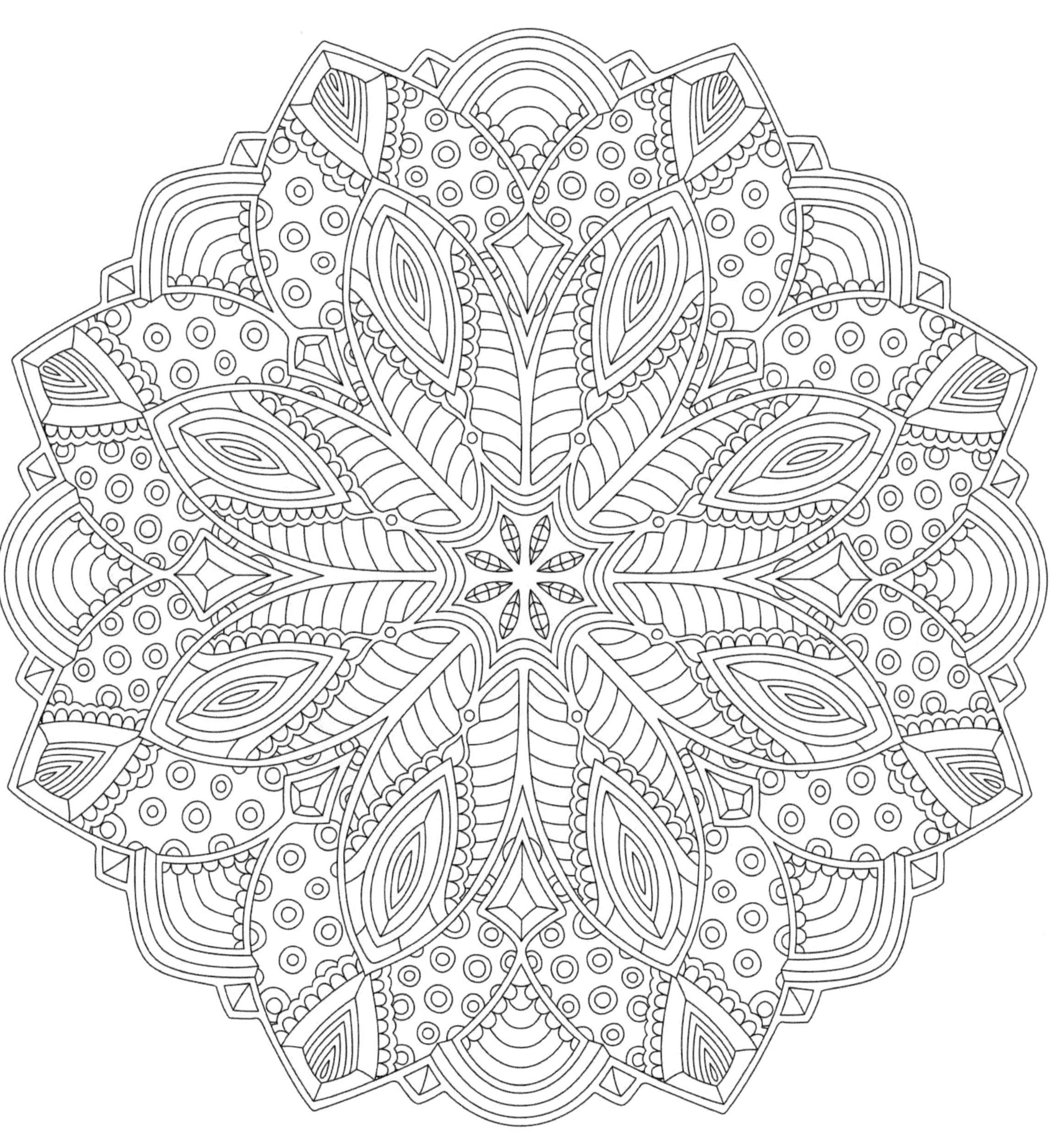

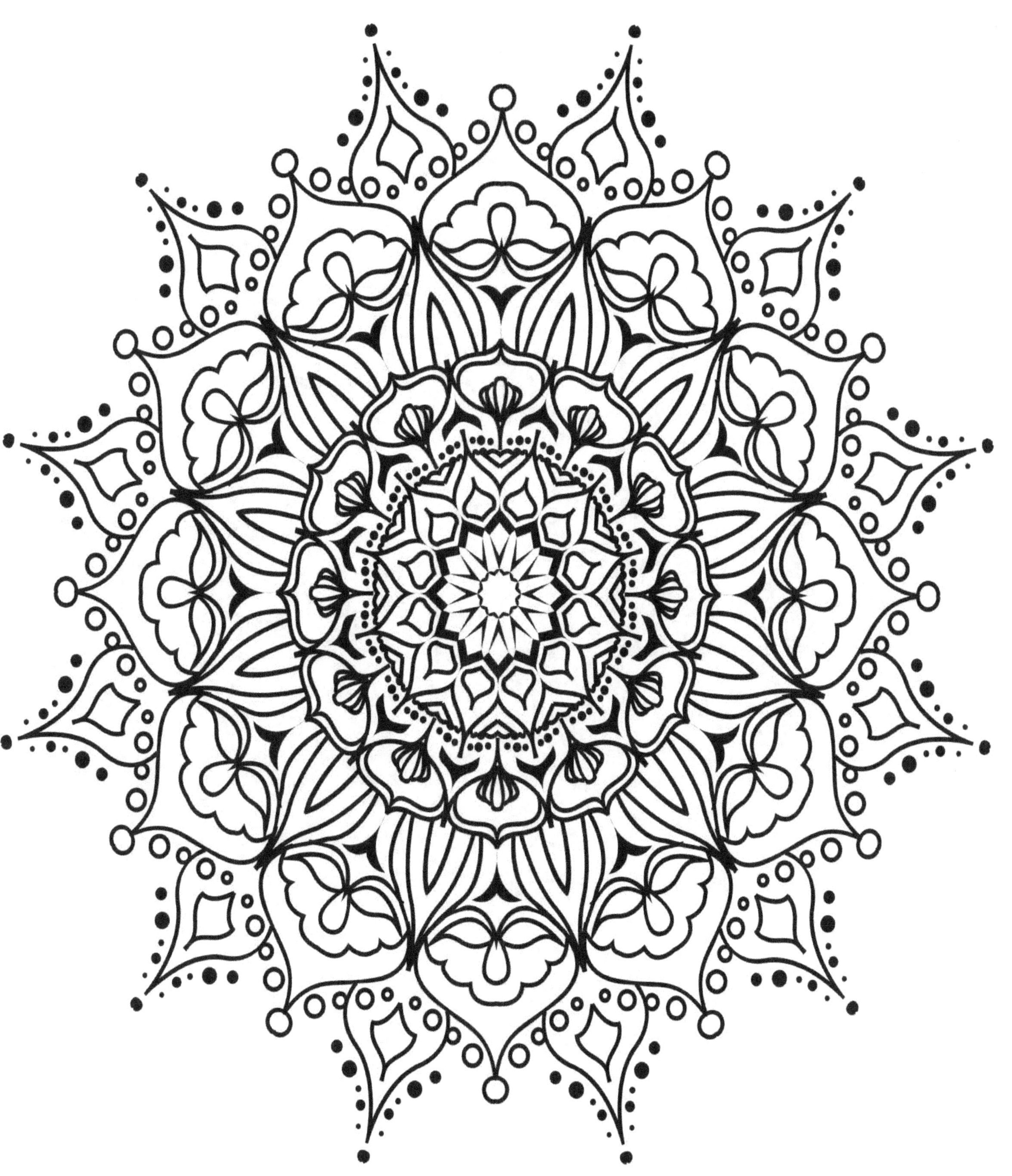

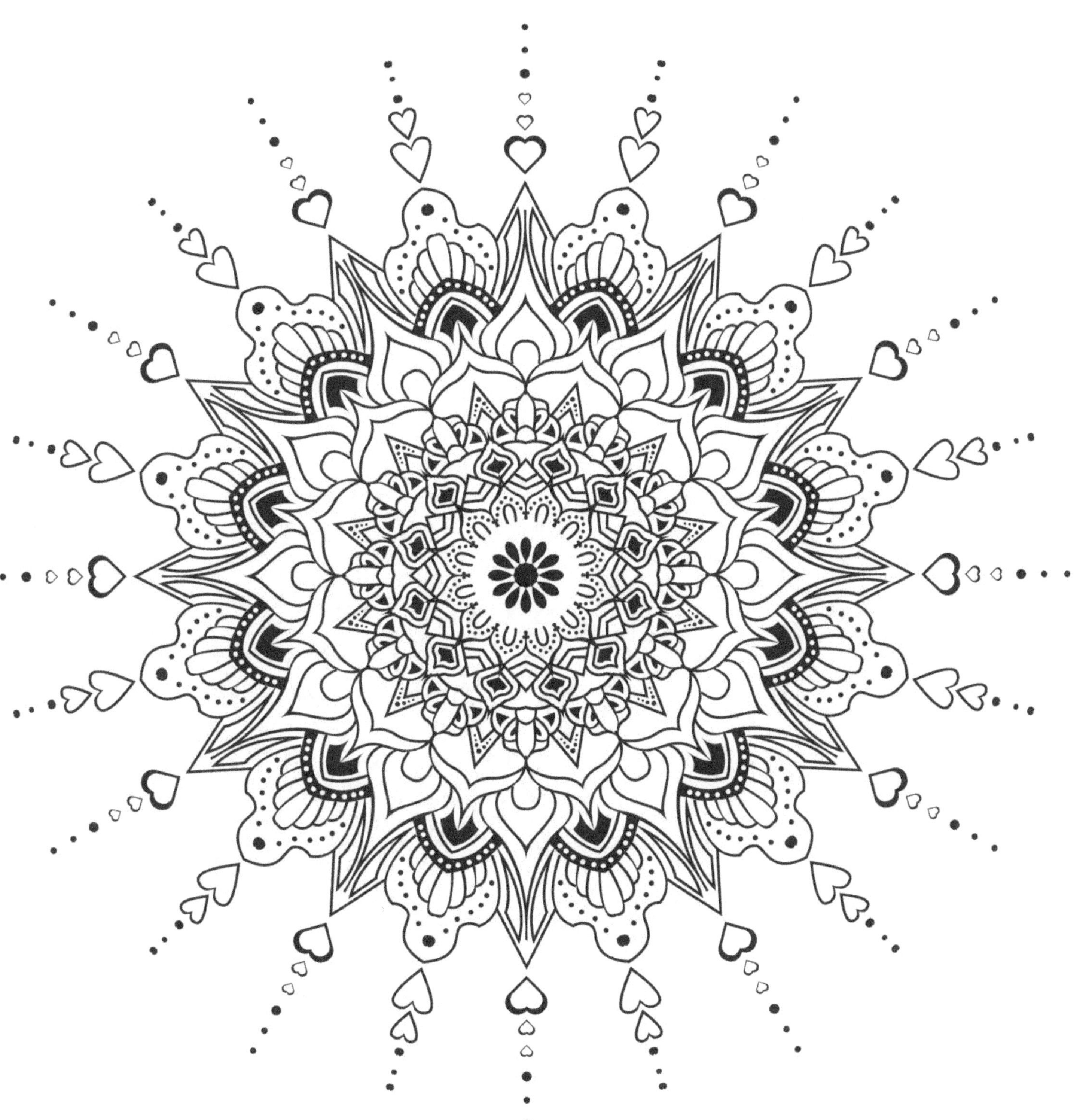

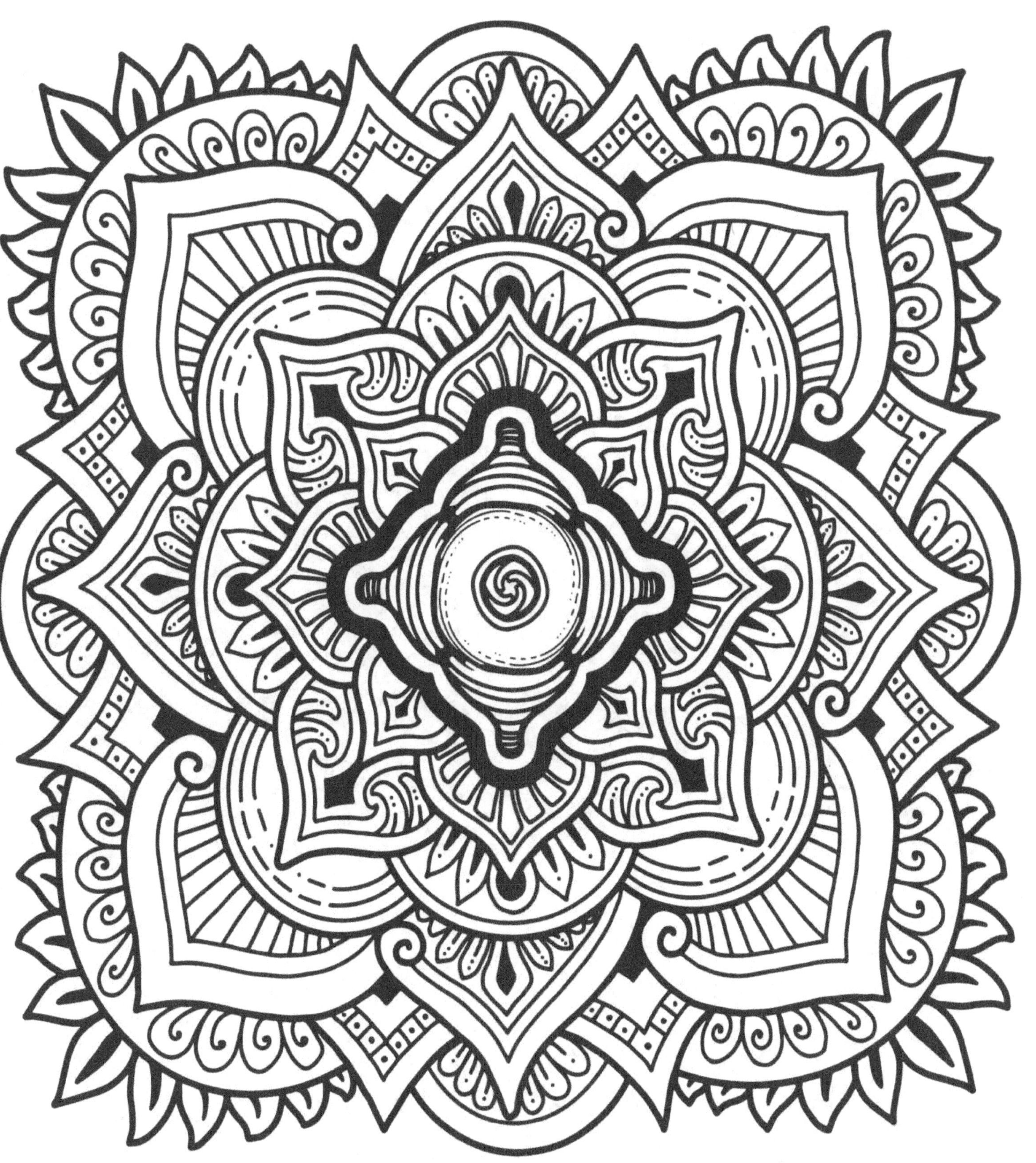

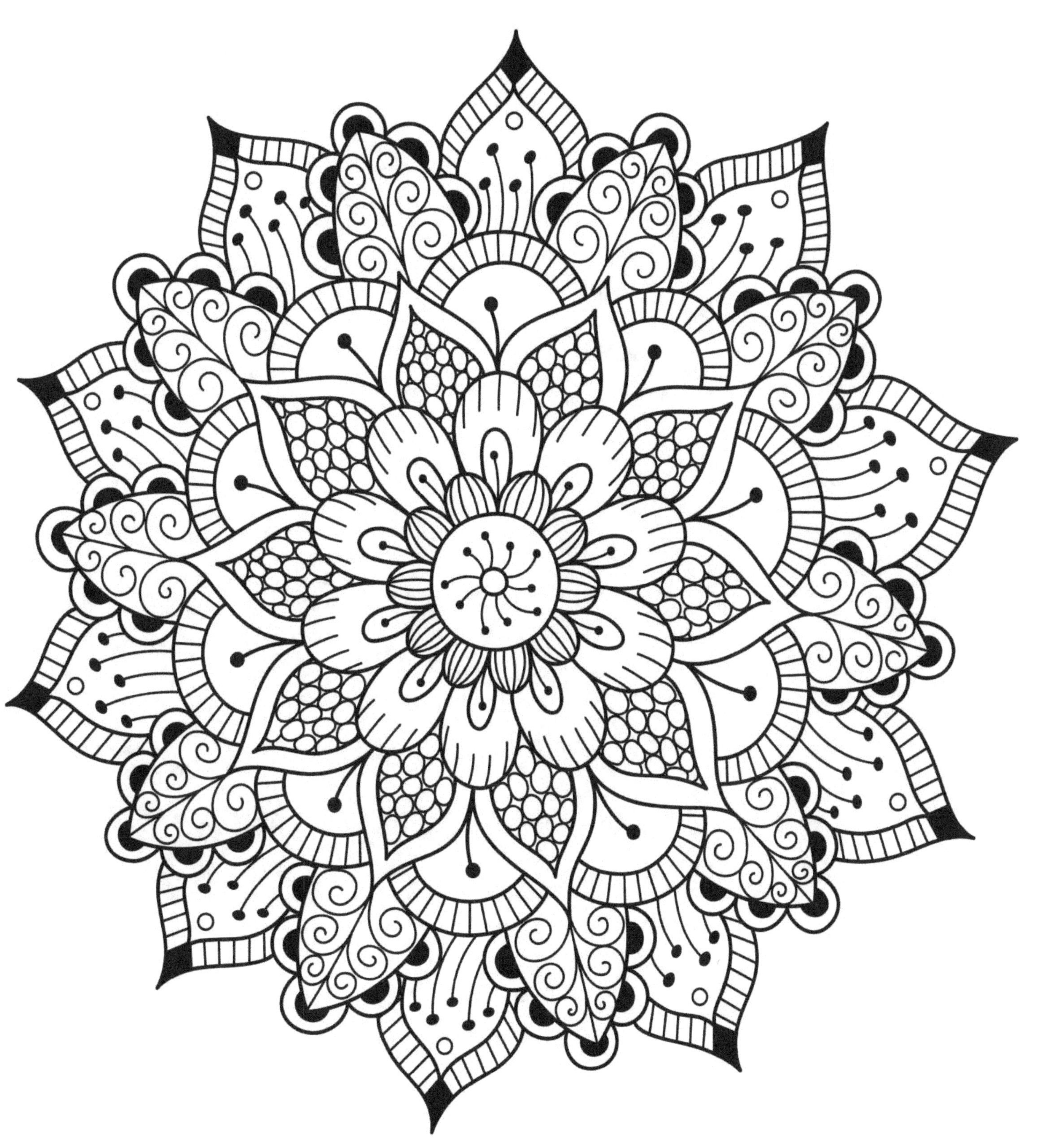

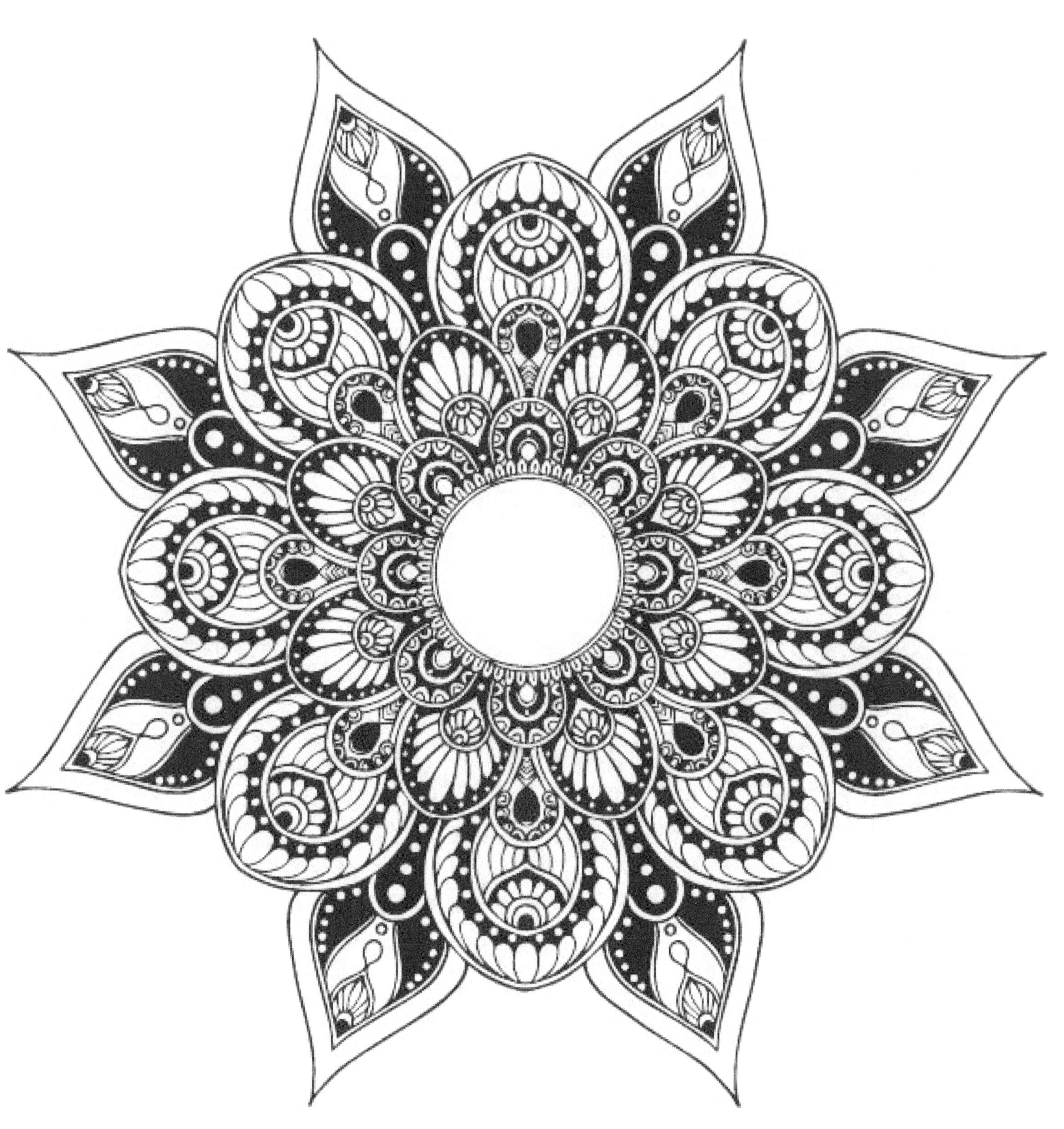

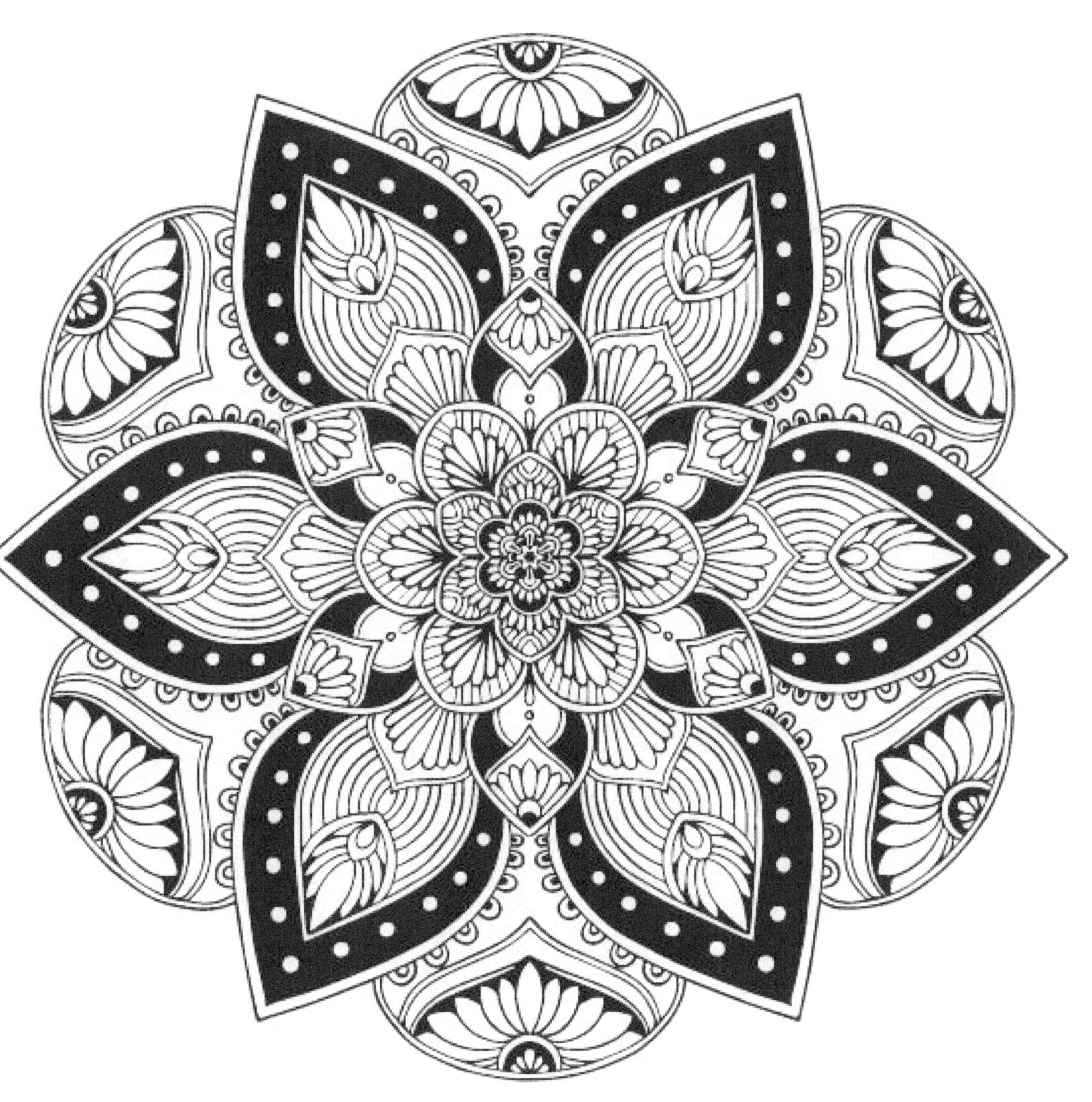

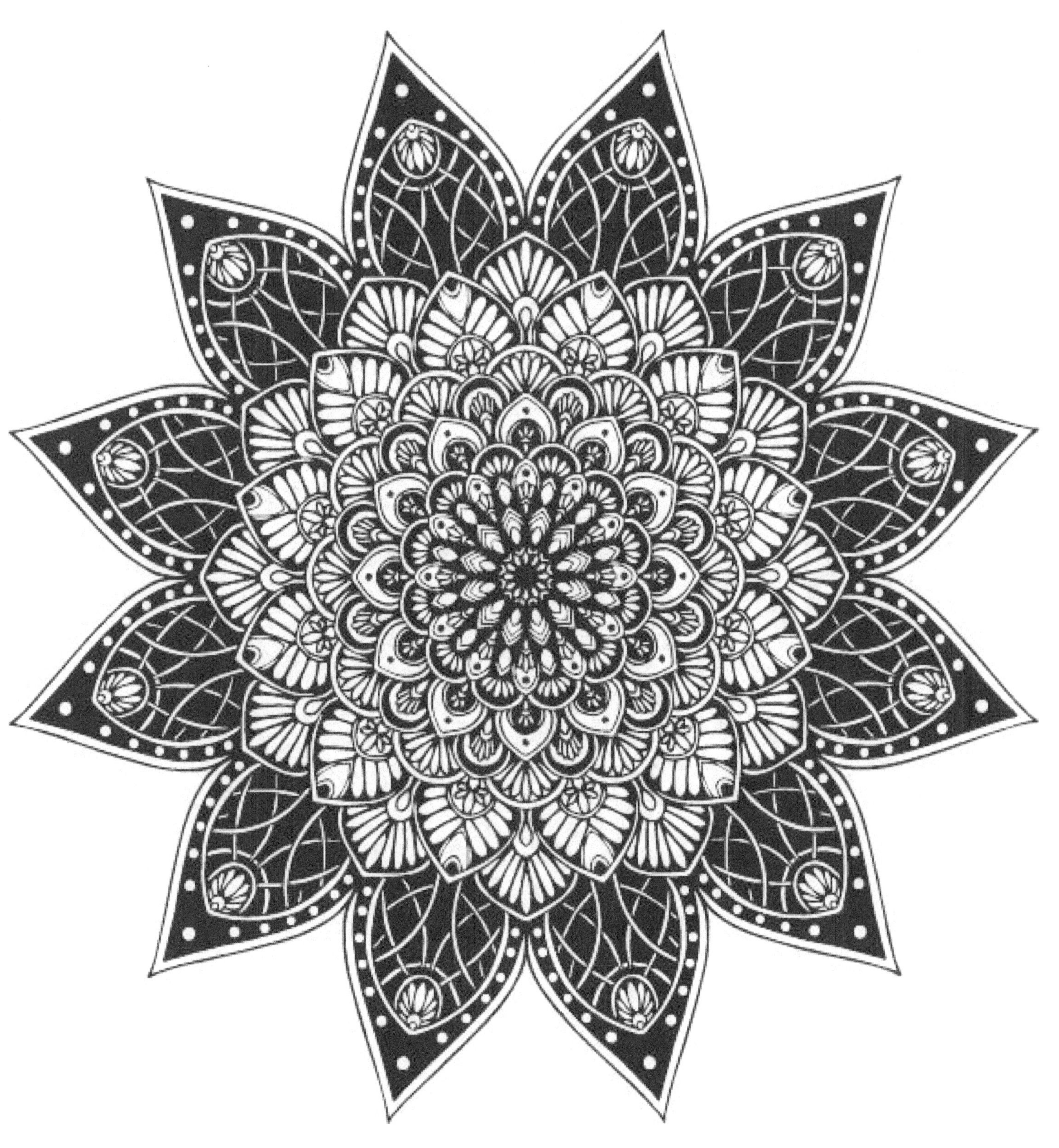

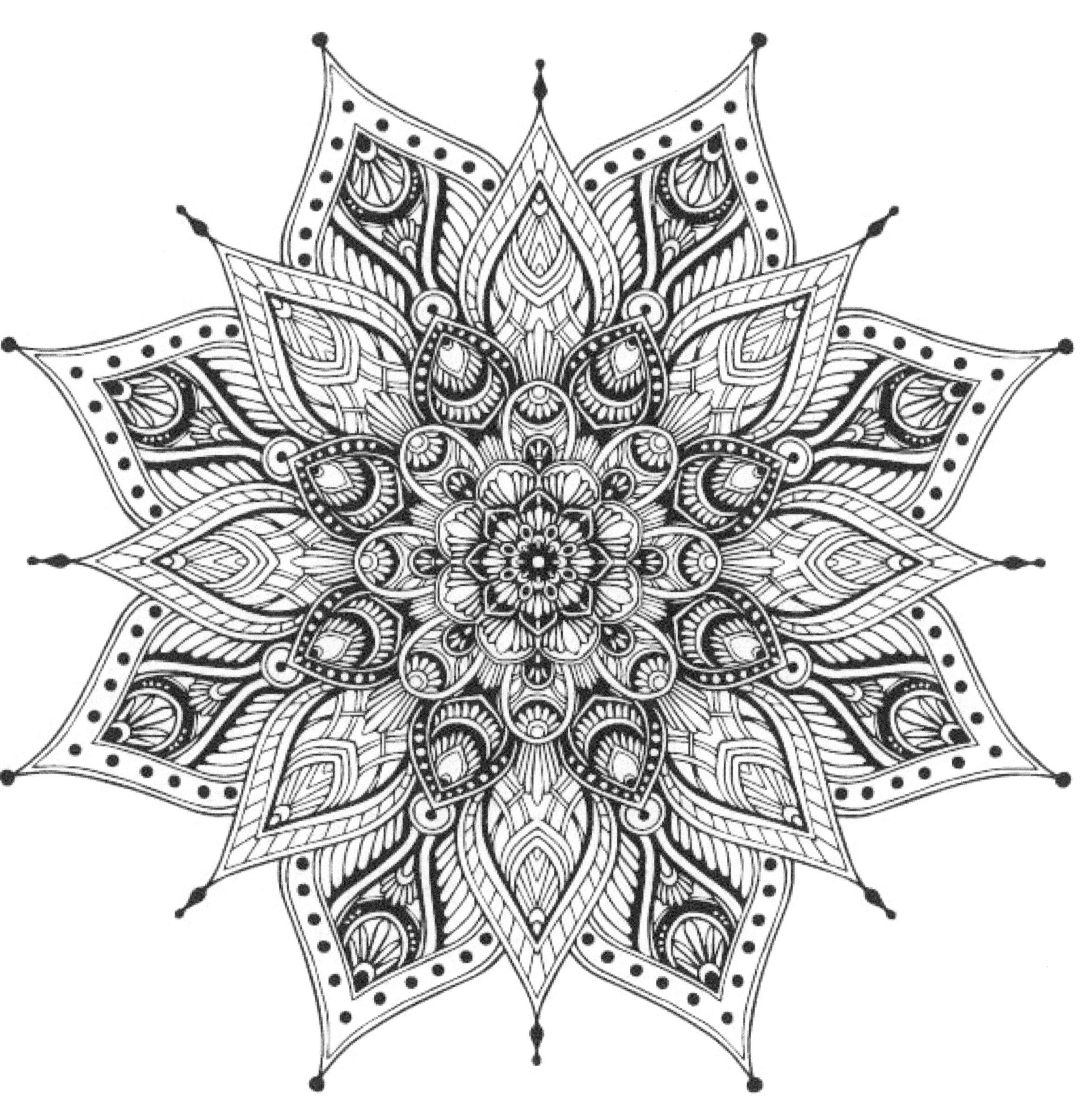

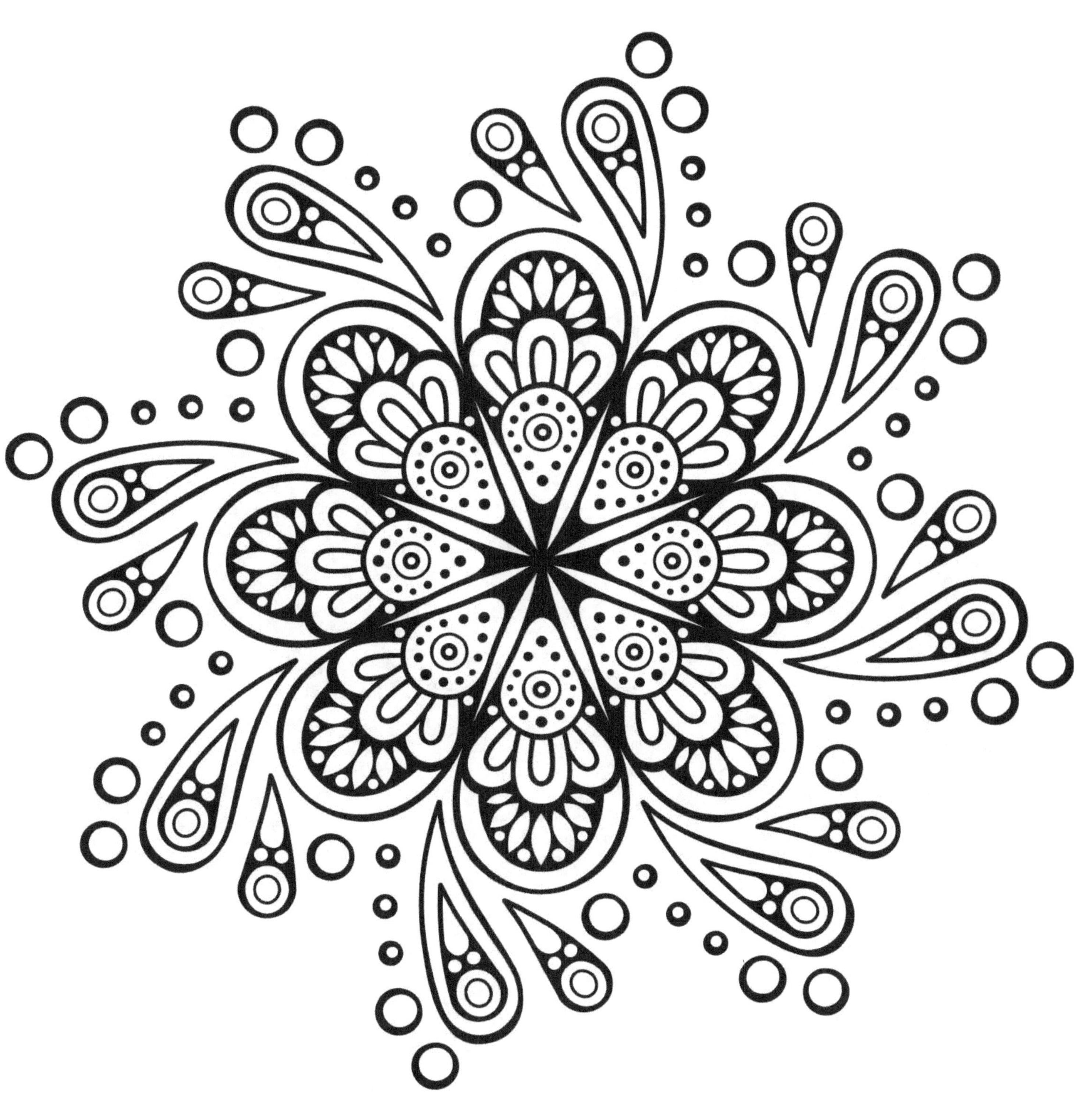

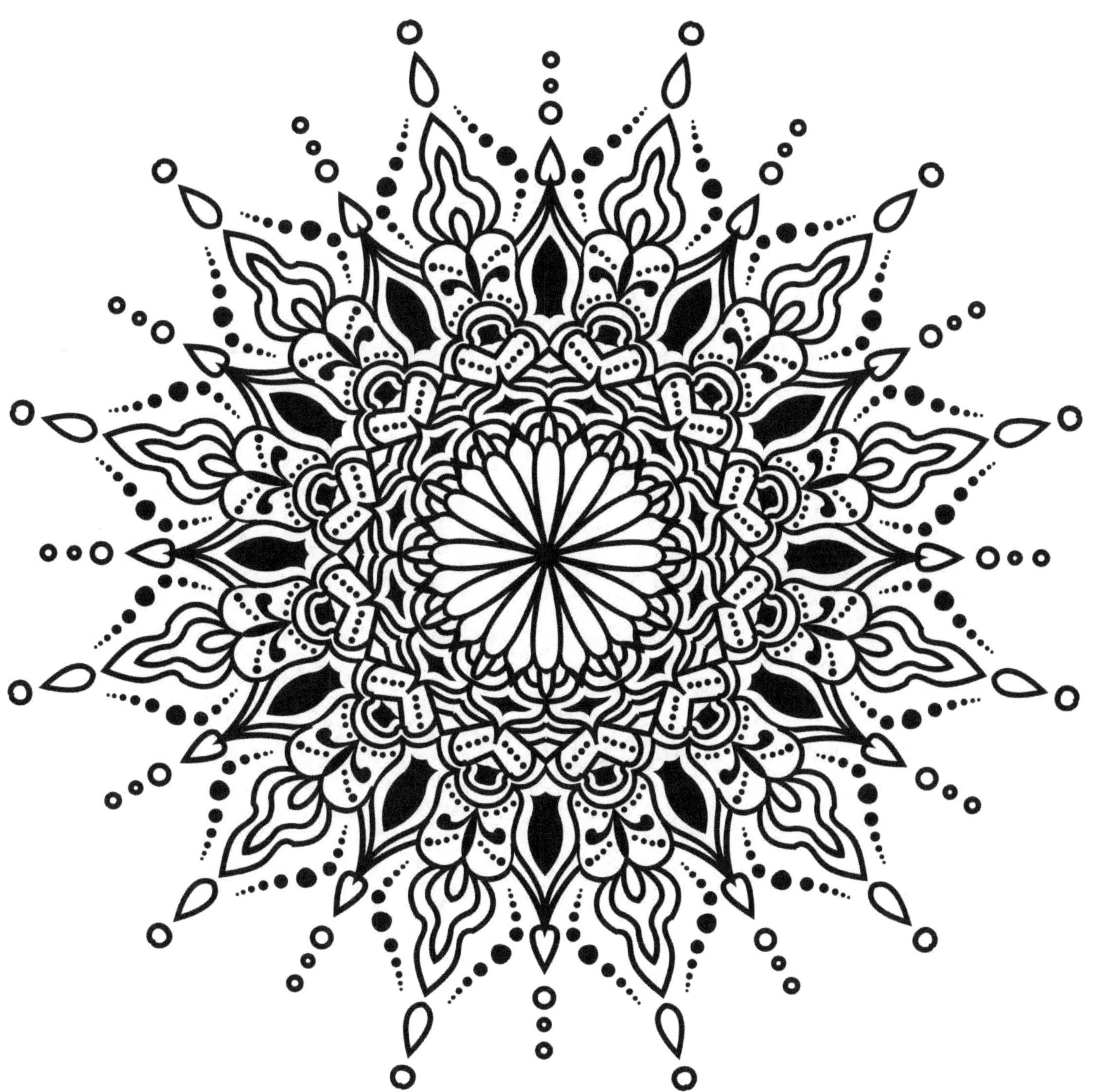

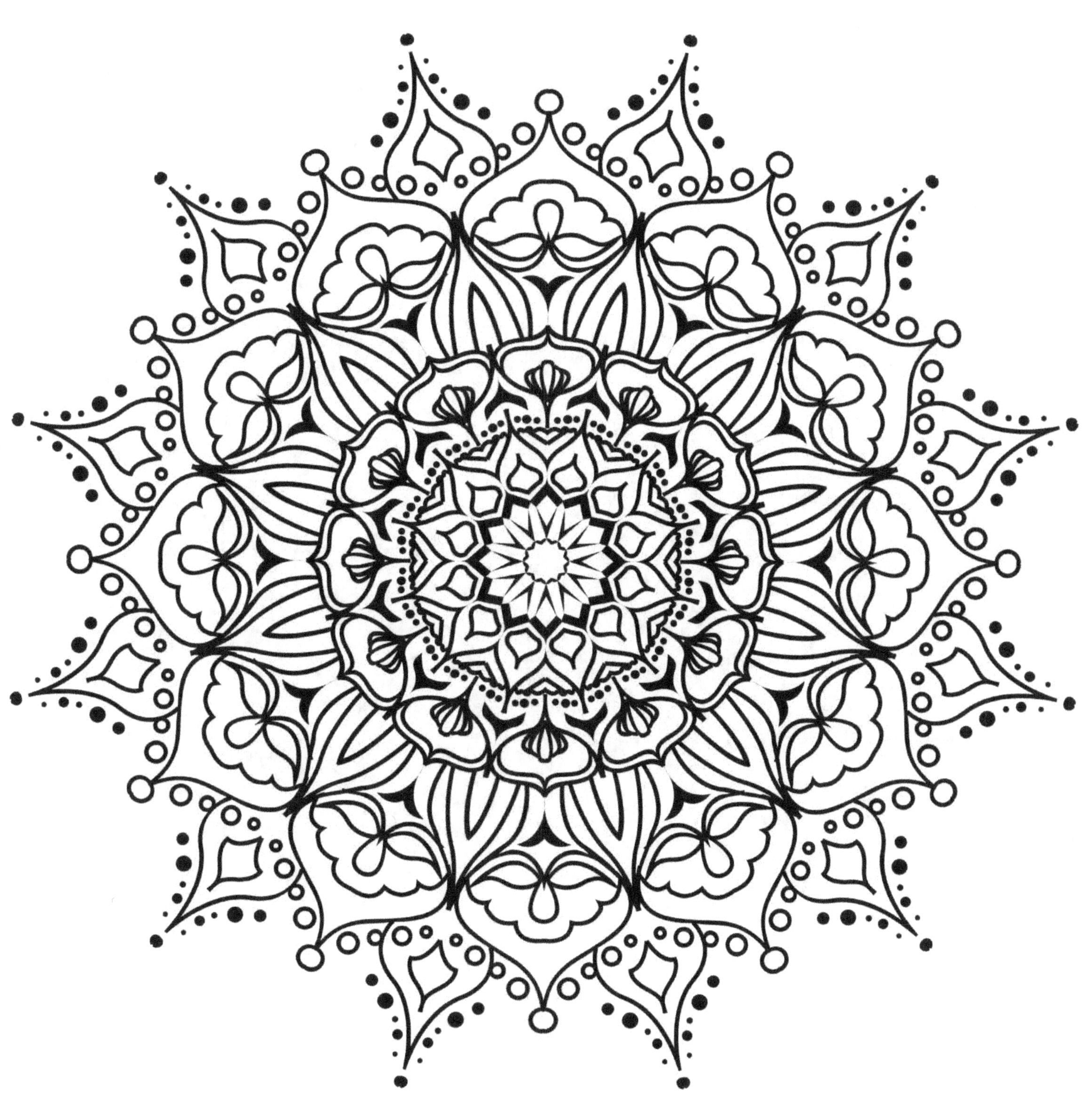

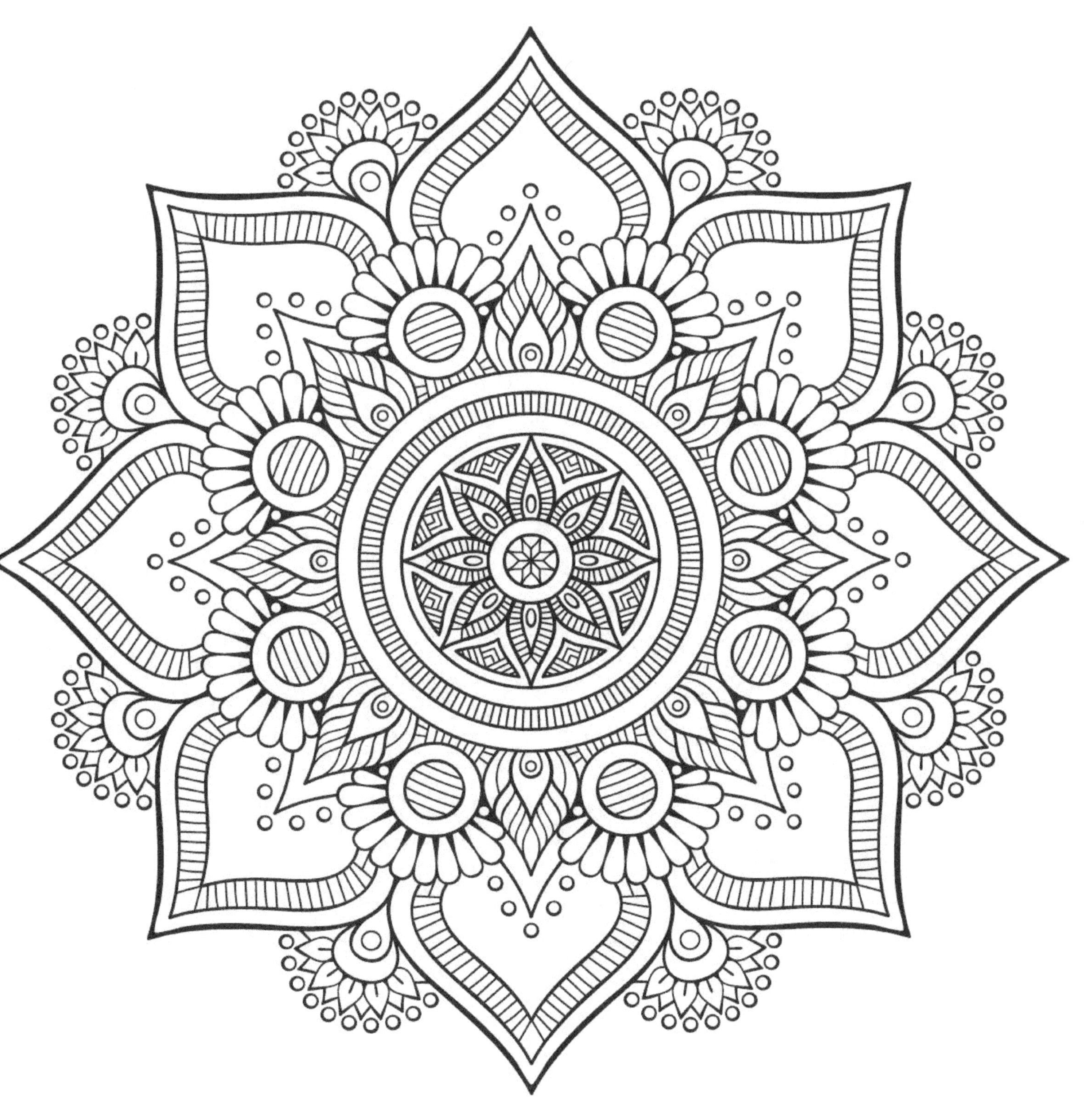

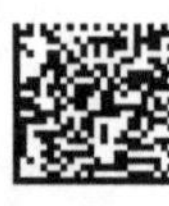

www.ingramcontent.com/pod-product-compliance
Lightning Source LLC
Chambersburg PA
CBHW081442250726
48662CB00009B/2914